THIRD EYE AWAKENING

*Unlocking the Power of Your Inner Vision
(2023 Guide for Beginners)*

Jasmine Chapman

TABLE OF CONTENTS

CHAPTER 1

THE THIRD EYE'S WORKING PRINCIPLES

The principles must be considered first when considering the third eye and their importance in unlocking our spiritual awareness. They are aspects we must comprehend in the future since they will serve as a light to our feet and a torch to our path. I'm sure you're wondering whether we're still talking about the same subject; trust me when I tell you we are since everything we've addressed here is about comprehension. These concepts would guide us and provide us with a clear perspective as we moved forward in this book and via our constant practices, rather than guessing. Let's get started, shall we?

Principle 1: Control of Force and Concentration

Any genuine spiritual practice is basically concerned with self-discovery. The main objective is to become much more. It is conceivable to hear that individuals only employ a tiny fraction of their potential. Their worlds are constrained within a tiny category, and they are often unaware of these restrictions in their thoughts, emotions, and other aspects of conscious existence.

If you have remained in a gloomy basement, this cellar is not a basement for you; it is the whole universe for you. You will never be able to understand the mystery that awaits you if you go out into the real world. This book's writing is all about leaving the basement and attempting to glimpse the magnificence of the cosmos via the third eye.

Developing your third eye is a proactive strategy to expand your conscious world and reveal your core principles in order to obtain insight into your own riddles. It's really rather simple. Simple may not necessarily imply simple, yet elaborate arguments or lengthy discussions are not required. Its advice is mostly philosophical and plainly more pertinent. Being is the finest thing on the planet. One recurring issue while creating this book was connecting theory to reality and providing tactics and keys to help you recognize yourself.

Before we begin the first process, let us provide some basic guidance on the principles and techniques of practice.

It is not necessary to be perplexed by the fact that our aim is a new insight or vision of the Self. The self is already waiting for you in the background. You will not "create" the Self and his aim; instead, you will expose it or allow it to show itself.

Spiritual development is undoubtedly a war, but the key weapon in that battle is to let go.

In this context of opening, it is unnecessary to concentrate, strive hard, or apply pressure. What may happen if you did? It implies that it is the part of you that you are conscious of right now - the conceptual mind that is continuously speaking in your thoughts. You were instructed to accomplish something from a young age. As a result, when you attempt to "do" the practice of perception, you will almost certainly stay in your speaking mind, which is intrinsically unsuited for all modalities of spiritual experience.

Begin doing it from there. You are aware, but you are just guessing. Allow that which is hidden in the depths to be revealed to your awareness. Allow things to happen without intervening.

In the real world, if you want something, you will battle for it. And, just as on the other side of the camera, everything is reversed in the metaphysical world. If you desire something, you must allow it to come to you. That is a new skill that must be developed. It might be referred to as "successfully letting go" or "creatively letting go." This is the capacity to be open and reveal layers of awareness via yourself. Take awareness seriously, and everything else will fall into place.

Principle 2 - Instead of attempting to be creative, just be aware.
It is advised that you never see or hear anything. That's fantastic if your vision is filled with images, colors, greater powers, or anything else. But don't attempt to cause it or invent it. Consciously picture no pattern in your thought field.

One reason is: Assume you truly have an elf come to you if you've been attempting to visualize the elves every day for a few weeks.

How will you know whether it's a true angel?
It is strongly advised that you never attempt to see or hear anything for yourself. That's fantastic if your

perception is filled with images, colors, greater powers, or anything else. But don't start it, and don't make it up. Consciously picture no trend in your thought field.

One reason is: Assume you truly have an elf come to you if you've been attempting to envision the elves every day for a few weeks.

How will you know whether it's a genuine elf?
This strategy should not be interpreted as a criticism of inventive imagery or imagination. There are various approaches to this.

It does not immediately apply to everything that is valid in a single growth system.

Principle 3 - Have Faith in Your Experience

It is critical to remember that if there is nothing to believe, there are no questions! Don't spend time thinking about what you think because you don't want to make it up. Have faith in your abilities.

Continue to concentrate on the balanced criteria, and your accuracy and dependability will improve. As you repeat these events, it becomes much simpler to trust them.

Principle 4 - Avoid Making Analogies During the Experience

When something happens, avoid attempting to assess it. Otherwise, you will completely lose your sight if you are immediately taken up in the linguistic mind. One of the keys to seeing the experience is the culture of prevailing quiet, the capacity not to react when anything happens inside.

After the event, you will have more than enough time to examine this. You won't get the most out of it if you test it or think about an event. Consciousness perceptions function similarly to seeds. It is only by patiently watching and digesting them that they develop.

Principle 5: Psychic Protection

Most individuals have two basic reasons for being mentally sensitive. First and foremost, they are unable to determine if they are dealing with negativity or whether vigilance is necessary. Second, they were not competent to seal their aura, making it impervious to outside forces if necessary.

As the body of implicit sensation and understanding, and as the key turn to the energy corpus, the third eye supplies the genuine solutions to each of these concerns.

First, it assists you in determining if your energy situation is sensible.

Our method of operation must be transparent, not just in terms of how to elevate your gaze, but also in terms of how to seal your aura. The vibration in the third eye begins with the very first tactic to awaken a higher density of guarding energy in the aura. The basis is a tangible comprehension of vibrating energy all around you, not a hopeful idea or self-sufficiency. You may use this protective energy not just in meditation, but also in the most diverse conditions of your life, such as busing, walking along a crowded street, or working with your boss or staff.

Principle 6 - Practice Consistently

Studying the book's contents without taking action is ineffective. **"Practice"** is the key to happiness in your spiritual path, whether you are poor or wealthy, stable or unwell. It is not necessary to sit and contemplate all of the time in order to acquire a high level of spirituality. You should read this book without spending more than 10-20 minutes a day meditating. However, you must include a variety of hobbies in your daily employment. Make them a habit and include this research in your daily routine as much as possible.

After considering several options, we often find that the procedure or manner in which research is conducted is not necessary. Your determination to proceed in one way makes a significant impact. When one considers the lives of many good rulers, one notes that they seldom begin at a higher level. They had to deal with considerably more formidable obstacles than you would encounter on your journey. They went so far that they could endure any obstacle, and huge illuminations appeared.

"Divine resilience" is one of the most essential qualities of a searcher.

people who have attained an exalted level of awareness without spiritual direction are often people who have lived long and arduous life. Performance comes from a constant devotion to all aspects of the practice, no matter how large you are.

What is the reason for the delay?

Begin the exercises while still reading the book. Tomorrow would never suggest personal growth. Do whatever can be done right now.

Experiment with the Practices

Because this is the greatest pleasure on Earth, countless enlightened men have sought inner calm. When you have dismal and utopian notions about spirituality, it completely fails you. The most educated instructors I know were men and women who shared a lot. If you play as hard as a child (and continue to do so), your chances are good.

CHAPTER 2

THE SECRET POWER OF THE LARYNX

Looking at another aspect of the skill of opening the third eye that we must master is the power of the larynx. This is a tremendous instrument that we must employ if we are to make any progress in our spiritual evolution. Let's go on.

Throat Friction

This method entails breathing with friction at the base of the neck while keeping the lips slightly open. Friction is created during inhalation and exhalation. It creates a 'wind' voice. There is no chirping, clicking, or chanting sound. When consuming and exhaling, the sounds are almost the same. If feasible, make it a low-pitched sound; it will be simpler to tolerate over time. Let me clarify a few points before providing further tips and guidance on throat friction.

Don't start looking for flawless friction in your throat. Simply create a specific kind' of friction and then let it calibrate to time.

If you try to do it properly, you can end up doing it all wrong. Being excessively gentle may hamper thinking. (The same can be said about all of the tactics in this book.) So simply inhale in the throat with a tiny pressure and everything will be OK! Only read the examples below, and you'll be able to return to this part in a few weeks to figure out where your friction is and modify the details in more depth.

Tips and Tricks

It doesn't matter whether you breathe via your mouth or nose at the same moment; nevertheless, your mouth must be open. The bottom jaw is relaxed and comfortable in this posture, resulting in a specific energy state and maybe a changed awareness.

Throat friction is more comfortable and effective when it emanates from the back of the throat rather than the lips or mouth, or near the teeth. If you produce your friction from the center or front of your mouth, the sound will be high-pitched and extremely near to whistling.

Experiment with everyone and compare the results.
The friction is created by the larynx as well as the underlying pharynx, which is located on the rear of the throat. more the tone would be lower, more passionate, and more absorbed than if it came from the lips.

Another possible failure is to produce pressure behind the internal nasal cavity from the upper pharynx, which implies on the back right at the top of the mouth. In an improper setting, pressure in the nasal cavity might echo rather than the pressure in the mouth.

You may also feel a quiet but distinct vibration in the larynx after performing throat friction by softly stroking your fingers on the apple of your Adam. In the first part, this noise is more clearly heard during inhalation than during exhalation, despite the fact that it is created throughout both.

How Profound Should Your Breath Be?

It should be standard in terms of scale and speed. Deeper breathing should be done at first to promote smoother friction. However, you do not have to gasp for air since this procedure does not generate the kind of breathing seen in rebirth. The idea is to use friction to activate the larynx power. It focuses on the oxygen larynx rather than respiration.

The objective of the neck pressure is to deepen your connection with **"power,"** a term that may sound unclear at first but becomes more vital as you continue to concentrate on your third eye. When you get used to this friction activity, you will only need to adjust your energy flow and will naturally obey the power of the atmosphere. Deepness and pace vary because the nature of strength differs, and our objective is to learn to flow with force.

When the spine is straight and erect, in accordance with the rest of the body, the robust action of this friction respiration may be greatly amplified. The more power the larynx releases, the higher the neck when totally straight. This may be sensed as a rapid increase in vibration, which usually occurs when the neck is gently adjusted, bringing it closer to optimal uprightness.

However, it is critical to ensure that the mouth is only partly open and that the bottom jaw relaxes appropriately so that the upper and lower teeth do not come into contact. Return to that spot whenever you are comfortable with the vibration between the eyes: attempt to exercise friction of the neck firmly in the mouth while partly opening the mouth.

When your lower mandible is comfortable and minimally dropped, you will notice a totally new energy state that increases the experience and stimulates a general release.

Beginners may perceive it as dry or moderately irritating to their throats. Reduce the pressure in the mouth if this is the case. Beginners typically raise the pressure in their mouth, which hurts their neck around the tongue. In any case, a few seconds of practice many hours a day will quickly alleviate this soreness. This conflict can be maintained humanely for hours. After a few weeks of exercise, the throat friction adjusts automatically and all unpleasant emotions fade.

It is vital to emphasize that this strategy concentrates on the larynx rather than the respiratory system. This cannot be regarded as a dehydration activity since the average strength is just the breath.

This is not even a respiratory workout in the traditional sense, since just physical air movement on the larynx is employed, with no effort to connect with the breathing cycle.

The pressure is employed to generate the feeling in the larynx, but at a later stage, the identical sensation in the larynx may be produced without the wind. Why is the Adam's Apple bulge on the larynx more prominent in men than in women? It was stated that Adam had a lump in his throat when he ate a bite of the wisdom tree's apple!

The Function and Effects of Throat Friction

The friction of the throat creates a tremendous vibration. When refined, it relaxes the mind and automatically develops a 'tuned-in' awareness. The advancement of psychological phenomena is a significant step forward. In the next chapter, we will connect your neck to the area between your brows to improve your third eye sensitivity. It connects the throat friction to various processes of the head chakra later in the workout to enhance it.

What Does "Connecting" Mean?

It's a feeling rather than a concept. Assume you attempt to connect the neck tension between the eyes. They are known at the start of the sequence. The two then spontaneously vibrate. The area between the brows vibrates in response to throat pressure. Then there will be mixing. The tightness in the neck combines with the feeling between the brows. This is what causes the energy exchange between the larynx, which results in the formation of the third eye. That is what "connecting" entails.

The following are the fundamental yet essential experiences: The comprehension of the third eye is readily clearer and quantifiable. It is an instant and direct result. The effect of throat friction is to morph,' to make the objects significant. When the throat pressure is linked to a chakra or another bodily organ, the organ becomes more quantifiable. The larynx exposes and then discloses things.

A similar effect may be seen when acting on auras. The inner environment must be built first, and then the quest process may begin. Several experiments next show how combining pressure and vision improves your knowledge of non-physical halos and auras. This is much 'denser' and more transparent to light and color.

The friction of the neck may also be utilized to link multiple energy systems. You may not only attach the friction to the third eye or another energy organ, but you can also increase the connection of other energy bodies and connect them through friction. In the channeling chapters, for example, you will attempt to link the energy of the hands with that of the third eye. Through the protection chapters, you will begin to connect the third eye and the belly energies.

As you go down this route, you will see a number of other fascinating aspects associated with the larynx. The energy larynx, for example, is a superb cleanser because it digests all kinds of harmful energies. The digestion of the nectar of life also plays an important function. It's not a common therapy for neck discomfort, I believe, but we consider it a spiritual search for the secrets of the larynx.

CHAPTER 3

AWAKENING THE THIRD EYE

Before we proceed any further, we'd want to clarify the concept of the third eye.

What exactly is the Third Eye?

The third eye serves as a portal between the realms of perception and the inner worlds. This is also the primary organ through which the body's awareness may be triggered and controlled. As a consequence, the third eye serves effectively as a key that may activate high frequencies of the energy system, resulting in higher consciousness states.

From a psychological standpoint, I've seen many individuals progress over the years as they converse with their third eye despite their difficulties. The third eye seems to convey a variety of energy motions as soon as it is activated due to its switch function.

It rapidly reverses a number of physical and mental disorders, which may be considered a kind of self-acupuncture. Furthermore, even before the third eye wakes, individuals seem to become more aware of deeper elements of themselves, which have a tremendous healing effect inside.

Naturally, I do not claim that referring to the third eye is required to cure anything, but the capacity of this facility is so large that I would not be shocked if more and more **"third eye"** remedies are developed in the next decades.

Texts equating the body to the temple may be found in both Religious and Buddhist traditions. If we made an analogy, we might compare the third eye to the temple entryway. You cross the bridge from the vulgar to the spiritual, from the stage when you read and write about your spirituality to the point where you begin to experience it. Those who have made themselves known as one of the most mystical items have always regarded the third eye, therefore the holy stone on the Hindu deity sculptures' foreheads.

In this chapter, we will discuss how a connection with the third eye might begin. Then we'll talk about a meditation practice that allows for further investigation and construction of the third eye.

The First Opportunity

Here are some things you should know before attempting the initial third-eye opening. This first exercise is designed to show you the very first 'line' for the third eye, as indicated by a feeling in the brows. It is designed to be conducted once or multiple times in a short period of time.

Instead, the eye practice will be combined with the breathing technique and other book activities. An easy method to get started is to choose a day when you have nothing planned, such as the beginning of a weekend.

Following this positive first impression, it is easy to grasp the remaining approaches.

You may undertake the exercises on your alone or with others to increase your strength. The day before the new moon is the ideal time of the month to launch. However, don't dwell too much on the present calendar. The secret is to do it rather than wait for the appropriate time.

Dress in light clothes.

You must struggle with a hazy understanding. You don't let the vibration in your skull sound like a knife. Even if just a tiny prickling sensation or tightness between the brows is detected, the procedure might begin.

Preparation

Find a quiet place where no one will bother you for at least an hour. You don't have to do it alone; you may do it with your friends as well. However, no one should be in the house who will distract you from your task.

- Light some candles all throughout the place. Remove your shoes.
- Remove your belt, scarf, or any clothing.
- Turn off your phone.
- Lie down on the grass, a rug, or a soft mat.

- You do not cross your arms but rather lay next to them. Palms facing up are preferable.
- Legs should not be crossed.
- Simply close your eyes. Please open your eyes. Keep your eyes closed until the session ends.
- Take 3 minutes to unwind.
- Make the sound for ten minutes.

Step 1

Become aware of your throat. Begin breathing with the pressure of your mouth. Maintain awareness of the feeling created by laryngeal pressure. Be aware without paying attention. Be mindful.

The energy is moving. Allow any movement of the body or awareness to occur. Continue to apply pressure for 5 to 10 minutes, keeping the larynx vibrating in mind.

Step 2:

- Maintain friction in the mouth.
- Instead of placing your awareness in the larynx, you now take notes between your brows.
- Don't concentrate. The cycle cannot occur if you grasp the region between your brows too tightly; the procedure would never occur.

- The flow of power. Obey what occurs to you on the spur of the moment. Follow your heart if your breath changes spontaneously and becomes stronger. However, keep some pressure in your mouth for the first five stages of the workout.
- For five minutes, remain just aware between your brows, inhaling through your lips. With this training period, precision is irrelevant, so don't glance at your clock.

Step 3

- Place your hand over your eyes in front of your face. It extends 5 cm (approximately 2 inches) from the palm and does not contact the surface. The face is unaffected by the palm.
- Sit for a few minutes on the ground with your eyes closed, breathing in the pressure of your neck between your brows and your palm, one inch above the air.

Step 4

- Place your palm in front of you or bring it back if desired.
- Close your eyes and breathe the pressure around your lips.

- Begin your search for a brow vibration. This might manifest as a strong feeling or numbness, or as a comparatively hazy tightness, weight, or brow heaviness.
- Don't push yourself too much. Allow things to happen and sit free.
- Keep your eyes closed at all times throughout this workout.
-

Step 5

- Continue as follows until the vibration, tension, severity, or weight of the slightest sense of vibration or tingling is observed: The brow sensation is connected to throat tightness.
- As you go, the relationship between the friction force and the third eye becomes clearer.
- When combined with friction, the vibration shifts. It is more subtle, but still fairly strong.
- Pay no attention to sensations or tingling in any part of the body, including the whole head, arms, or chest. Keep your eyes open and aware of the vibration.
- This technique is repeated for around eight minutes by connecting to the throat friction and increasing the vibration between both brows.

- It entails integrating the tension and vibrations of the brows at the same time.
- There is no imagination or originality. Flow solely with what comes your way.
-

Step 6:

- Do not massage your throat.
- Don't pay any further attention to the noises.
- Keep your eyes closed and only be aware for ten minutes or longer between your brows.
- Stay completely motionless and feel the power that surrounds you. It seems that the faster you get, the more in tune you are.
- Take note of any light or color movement between the brows.

Suggestions and Tricks

Do not fixate or 'grab' the region between your eyes; instead, maintain your attention on it very little. Clutching just stops the cycle. Allow things to happen without intervening.

Focusing on the eyes simply means being aware of the location and twisting the head as if trying to look at it. Stress would only disrupt the regular path of your experience if you added these ocular movements. As a result, the eyes are not led in any particular way—this is consistent throughout the text.

At first, a characteristic feeling is a vibration felt not just between the brows but also elsewhere on the front or neck. When this happens, concentrate only on the feeling between the brows and connect it to the pressure in the neck. All of this must be implemented in practice.

If you practice with mates, avoid making contact with each other to avoid needless energy transmission. If the experience is too intense, all you have to do is open your eyes and return to normal awareness.

Various Experiments

If you grasp this first opening, the only thing that matters is the contact between both brows and the beam. The ideal method is to disregard any additional indicators that may appear during functional implementation.

If the third eye and astral energies are dealt with, there may be little indicators, such as twitching in the body and memories returning to the mind, at first. Allow them to come and go since they don't signify anything. Ignore the protocol as if nothing has occurred.

The pressure, squeezing, force, or light you feel between your brows might be intense, but it doesn't matter whether they are smooth or smudged. As we shall see later, an individual's energy level varies dramatically from one day to the next, thus it is possible that you attempted the first opening' on a lesser-intensity day. Such features no matter how little, constitute a key thread, and a systematic technology is gradually used to transform the book into a simple third-eye comprehension.

What If You Don't Feel Any Vibrations?

Here are a few pointers for folks who don't feel anything between their brows throughout their exercise. The experience exists and is not rare, although it cannot be documented.

Perhaps something extraordinary or really powerful is in the works. If it's too basic, you probably didn't give it much thought. This sound is always between your eyes. Perhaps your efforts are blocking the operation. Allow things to happen without focusing. Allow it to come to you; don't even seek your vibration. Maintain the workout, but let go.

There is an explanation for why you don't feel any vibration: light may be used instead of vibration. Remember these quick references: When you see the light in some form, you have entered the heavenly realm and are no longer in the physical realm. It is impossible to be both outdoors and inside a home at the same time. And if you acquire light, you're extremely likely to overcome the vibration level. It begins with light rather than a vibration in this case. In the form of meditation, go from step 2 to step 3. Don't focus on the vibration; instead, connect the neck pressure to the light.

More information about the Third Eye

An essential proposal is to utilize the eye as a forehead mark or as a coin. The third eye is more of a duct or tube that connects the area between both brows to the bone behind the ear.

Tunnel of the Third Eye

Along the tunnel, there are a number of power centers that enable you to speak with other worlds and levels of consciousness.

This explains why multiple systems can detect the third eye: As a starting point, they would each choose a certain core along the pipe or even an energy source perpendicular to the tube.

The materiality of the third eye is important to highlight. The majority of the third eye is an astral body energy system or surface of life force. Because the astral body has numerous relationships with the physical body, the third eye is also strongly associated with several human bodily components, such as pituitary glands. This is the most important transformation for an astral body.

However, other writers believe that assuming the third eye is the pineal or hyperphysical gland is too simple. As previously stated, the tube in the third eye is not exterior.

It has an impact on the body's biological systems, including the cortical sinuses, optic nerves, cribriform plate nerves, frontal sinus glands, pituitary and endocannabinoid receptors, the center of the cortex, and the pulmonary veins. One of those interior structures would be too ambiguous and limited to be referred to be the third eye. Again, it is a strength organ; the third eye does not exist. It may have an exclusive relationship, but it cannot be limited to any of them.

At first, don't concentrate on anything else in the passage; just be aware between your brows. You have to start somewhere, which is the fantastic advantage of producing good energy in the environment around you when your brows stimulate this specific core. Additional 'pipe' centers would be built subsequently.

This suggests that the whole third eye is not the area between the brows. However, it is the surroundings that we must employ and set as the key switch in the early phases of our activity in order to be constantly conscious of. You don't want to suppress sensations in particular portions of your brain, but you're also not paying attention. Maintain your focus between your brows.

Meditation on the Third Eye

Let's get started with our main meditation practice. The early stages of the meditation cycle are not designed to rocket you into wonderful levels of spirituality, but rather to gradually and finally develop a third eye in order to reach perfect inner calm. One common misconception is that you cannot battle your thoughts psychologically. It's difficult to calm the thoughts. It is, nevertheless, conceivable to build a system outside the mind that can govern the mind.

Preparation

Take off your socks, jacket, scarf, and jewelry.

Sit with your back straight and your legs crossed on the ground or on a chair. You do not have to be on the board, but it is quite evident. It is preferable to sit on a chair without pushing against it, allowing energy to circulate.

Step 1: Laryngeal Energy

- Close your eyes for a moment. Keep your eyes closed until the meditation is over.
- To breathe, use your throat pressure.
- The friction's breathing generates throat waves. Maintain awareness of the feeling in your larynx. Friction is used to enhance laryngeal vibration.
- The throat feeling is divided into two parts: One actual, caused by the physical movement of breathing, and another subtler, like a picking, always felt after respiration stops.
- Use throat friction to cause another irritation. Adjust your backbone role to get the full impact. Align your neck so that it is absolutely symmetrical with the rest of your body. Check that your neck, arms, and the rest of your back are all straight.

- See if you can enhance the feeling of the larynx and the energy flow in the neck by going as close to a vertical position as feasible.
- Maintain as much stillness as possible.

Step 2: Vibration in the Eye

- Continue to breathe with friction in the throat, but let the throat awareness to fade. Keep an eye on the brow vibration.
- Connect the vibration of the eye to the pressure in the throat.
- If you're not sure what connecting means, simply keep both the neck pressure and the brow vibration in mind. It would soon become evident that there is a link between the neck and the head. That is what it means to connect.
- Step two involves amplification with throat friction to augment and intensify the vibration of the eye.
- Tingling is an option if you prefer hefty volume versus soft plucking. Keep the light feeling going.

Step 3: Let There Be Light in Your Eyes

- Maintain the throat friction.
- Take away vibration awareness. Look for a haze, a sheen, or any kind of illumination or color

between the brows. All of them may be seen as different light modalities, which in this book, of course, refers to spiritual, not material, with eyes closed.

- Remember, there is no creation, no imagination, simply curious about what is ahead.

- If any of these light modes are regarded as blurry, attribute it to throat friction. Similarly, to how the friction was connected to the vibration between your brows in step two, the tension was now linked to the light. Instead of intensifying the sound, you are now attempting to enhance the light.

- As you work, you will see brighter and lighter regions of light. The understanding of the hazier areas gradually diminishes in order to concentrate on the most vivid. Connect the amplifier's friction to the light component.

- The little, brilliant light molecules that travel in various directions across space across from you are well-known phenomena.

- When friction is combined with these light waves, you will be given helpful energy; a few will enter you and then go directly into your core.

Step 4: Space Awareness

- Keep your head between your brows.

- Instead of concentrating on the light itself and its brightening components, consider the light backdrop. The blackness at the base of all the hues gives you a feeling of the space ahead of you.

- Space might seem either violet or black. The sense of space is more significant than the hue.

- Maintain a sense of distance. Allow it to devour you.

- At this time, throat friction may be lessened or even eliminated. When the mind wanders to emotions, breathe with friction once again.

Step 5: Spin Around in Space

- Begin spinning in space, spiraling forward and clockwise in front of you, as if you were slipping down a tunnel.

- Spin around like you're caught in a whirlwind.

- In the vacuum, the vortex awaits you. Try not to create a wave that will send you plummeting. Allow the vortex to grasp you and guide you through its typical course.

- As you go, the quality and color of the environment will change, as if you were projecting into a whole other place.
- Recognize the many emotions and stay up with the vortex.
- You may employ the throat friction to accentuate the vortex effect on a regular or even continuous basis.
- Get rid of any worries about your breath, your head, or the room... Take control of your eyes.
- Because you are decreasing your awareness, you are unable to act. You should not even be aware of yourself.
- Maintain complete stillness. It is possible to learn to let go.
- Allow awareness to grab control of the head.
- Bring your attention back to your eyes. Pay attention to the noises around you.
- Maintain bodily alertness. Take a few deep breaths.
- Take as much time as you need to return completely, then press the fingers of your right hand and open your eyes.

Step 1: Tips (Larynx Vibration)

- Even if it is difficult to distinguish between physical and non-physical oscillations at first. The system must continue on its course in order to get a hazy grasp of the feeling, both physically and intellectually. By striving to be exact, the mind may get in the way and hinder the process.

- Anything related to vibration would be easier after applying the channel release procedures.

- To increase the energy experience, place your hand near your chest, approximately one inch away, at first. This will not be required subsequently.

- As with any laryngeal function, it is critical for the spine to remain as upright as possible throughout this process.

- What are the key differences between animal and human bodies? One key distinction is that humans are vertical, while animals are mostly horizontal.

- Similarly, although though these animals have a larynx, it is not vertical.

- This sheds light on the relevance of linearity in the setting of the larynx. Another tip is to consider what happens in the first phase of the meditation: The feeling in the larynx abruptly increases when you reach a fully upright posture of the spine.

Step 2: Tips (Vibration in the Eye)

- The force larynx is a modulator and form patron. When you correlate the area between the eyes with throat pressure, you try to establish the third eye.
- The feeling in the eye becomes more intense when linked to the rubbing and movement of the larynx, according to experience.
- As previously explained, the feeling might be sensed as a throbbing, tension, or force. This method is utilized to produce the astral layer of the third eye.

Step 3: (Light in the Eye)

- At first glance, it seems that you can only detect light in the eye while experiencing throat friction. It is consequently unavoidable that a contact occurs in order to send the energy created by the throat friction to the light-perceiving region of your third eye. In exercise, the experiment was quite simple: The pressure seems to "puff" the light, making it more visible and brighter, which is another way to 'shape' the larynx.

- Many students who believe they can't "see the light" see it but don't know what it is. You must agree that the impression of lighting may be faint at first, like a fuzzy white haze, and that the first thread is this weak light.
- Use the larynx amplification effect to enhance it. The little light and practice is an awakening.

Step 4: (Space) Hints

- When it comes to the perception of black space, a common experience is an overpowering sense of relief in your heart, as if you have suddenly taken up a big weight. The heart feels incomparably lighter as you reach the inner vacuum.
- The position of the clock should not be taken on a regular or as-needed basis.

Step 5: Tips (The Vortex)

The clock's orientation should not be considered uniform or necessary. As always, you must be aware of the energy of the moment, which often causes you to reverse and reverse. When there is no wind, it is preferable to take a step forward and go in a clockwise manner.

The vortex is a jumble as well as a tube. It is simpler not to have predetermined norms of feeling. Allow the understanding to grow gradually on its own.

Rolling through space is a dynamic science of vortexes from which you may travel across time and space. This adds a trip that is not designed to project itself outside of the body, but rather travels so deep within that almost nothing remains. ISIS makes extensive use of the vortex phenomenon, which goes from one space-time to another.

Approach the vortex with amazement and interest, as it will transport you into an astounding enigma where you will encounter riddles billions of years older than you.

Thoughts During Meditation

During meditation, ignore your emotions and just follow the processes. You will quickly realize that a strong pulse between the brows helps to calm the mind and substantially decrease the present flow of emotions. There is no need to fight ideas mentally. Don't pay attention to them. Just don't pay attention.

You just close your eyes and begin the exercise whenever you are sidetracked by a question. Thinking will become less difficult when the third eye develops throughout the cycle. After some degree of development, the third eye provides the capacity to completely get out of the mind and hence from thinking.

If the frequency of thought is disrupted, you may sometimes calm them down by increasing the pressure in the neck, which increases the vibration within the eye. But keep in mind that our meditation tries to build the third eye, which is a notoriously useless practice. After then, ideas are mostly irrelevant.

Time Estimates for Each Step

- Thirty minutes of meditation for each of the five phases: Each of them takes five minutes, plus five minutes for each stage.
- For the next 60 minutes: Step 1 takes 5 minutes. Step 2 takes 10 minutes. Ten minutes for the third phase. The fourth quarter will last 10/15 minutes. The fifth level takes 20 minutes. 5 minutes over the head.
- Take around 2 minutes for each phase in a ten-minute meditation.

Step 1 is an important aspect of the procedure and should not be overlooked, despite its small length.

The humming sound is used in this manner. Sit up straight with your back straight and your chest sound. In stages 1–3, use humming instead of pressure in the mouth to produce the third eye visualization.

So, as in Phases 4 and 5, allow oneself to enter space with stirring noises on occasion.

Tip

These soothing sounds provide you a strong technique to project into space. Do not be afraid to contact them if your meditation is disrupted by emotions or cognitive events.

CHAPTER 4

SEEING

Seeing is one of humanity's best qualities. This is a fantastic excursion that will help you comprehend your own vastness. Naturally, there are increasing levels of eyesight.

The primary difference between these two perspectives is that in the former, ideas are confined to the subconscious. One of the keys is to be less concerned with what you see in order to get a glimpse of reality and more interested in observing experience and enabling the mind to grow through seeing. Then you have a whole new perspective and understanding of the world.

Because perception overpowers the mind's expanding thinking, it is impossible to adequately translate what is seen into words. That is why true vision feeds the intellect while disproving the soul's erroneous beliefs. Seeing must be seen as a transformative experience rather than just a method for perception. Seeing is a more expansive style of perception.

One of the most typical beginner mistakes is believing that their regular eyesight and normal eyes would perceive supernatural facts as if they were instantaneously incorporating auras and heavenly beings into the world pictures that they get. It is unable to operate since it is the blind component of regular cognitive awareness. To begin seeing, get out of your head since it is the most important thing.

As a result, one of the chapter's recurring teachings is to stop seeking if you want to see. That is, avoid storing and evaluating visuals in the same way that you do your ideas. You don't want to see it. When you attempt, you work from your subconscious. enable yourself to enter another state of consciousness and enable something else to happen. The next step is to get beyond representations and experience non-physical experiences in normal cognitive awareness. In order to achieve this goal, a number of eye contact tactics will be used. It may be done with a partner or alone in front of a mirror. Both have advantages, and I recommend that you do both.

Eye Contact Behaviors

- The two people must not be sitting too far apart. A distance of 3 feet is ideal. If you can't strike the other person's face with your hand, you've come a long way. When you look in the mirror, your reflection may seem to be within the same range or somewhat farther away.

- A white wall as a background is still preferable for saving energy when using candles.

- Because the two people's eyes must be on the same level, cushions for adjustment are used if one person is taller than the other.

- You may be sitting, but your spine should be straight. Do not support the free flow of energy by leaning against a door or the end of a chair.

Connect to Space Again

- Before making any eye contact, the following behaviors begin to reconnect with the eye: Close your eyes and sit up.

- Begin the friction in the throat.

- Recognize the vibration and connect it to the throat friction between both brows. Continue to make the vibration between your eyelids for around 1 minute.

- Take note of any changes in lighting or color. Connect your throat pressure to the light. Continuously for 2 minutes.

- Be cautious of dark space (background light and shadow).
- Stay in space for 2 minutes. This set of instructions is a condensed version of the previously described third eye meditation.
- The eye refers to the third eye, not the physical eyeballs behind the brows.

Eye Contact in Relation to Eye Concentration and Vision

- Let us start with the first two parts of our three-part vision cycle.
- Sit with your back straight in front of a companion or a screen.
- Please shut your eyes for three minutes to reconnect.
- Then you should open your eyes. Turn your head toward a mirror or your friend's gaze.

Part 1: Stuck Focusing on the Eye

Make yourself mindful and really steady between the brows. Act in immobility, which is more than just a lack of movement. By focusing on the hand, it's all within, as if the blood were congealing. You can tell you're becoming fatter.

The quiet of the eye is a 'connected silence,' which allows you to feel the power of the eye echoing throughout the whole body.

As a result, the body perceives higher density or increased frequency. When you reach the pinnacle of quiet, you feel as if you can't move. In actuality, if you actually needed to, you would. However, in order to do so, you must first gain comprehension.

When the term "third eye" is used in the book, it refers to the area between the eyes. However, keep in mind that "focusing between your brows" will just keep you conscious of this region. This is not intended to direct your eyes while attempting to look between your brows. The eyes are not very concentrated, and in fact, the more you can ignore them, the better. This is true for third-eye meditation, in which the eyes are closed, as well as eye contact activities.

Part 2: Consciousness 'Seeing'

The tremendous mystery of the seers emanates from here, and huge sight openings may result. When you focus your attention on an item with your eyes open, you typically look at the image in its many sections. The conscious mind then analyses the various components. Many ways for improving mental awareness also teach you how to extract more information from an image than ever before. For example, you will be given a draft of multiple things. There is a brief opportunity to inspect it for a few seconds.

Then you might say anything your subconscious is actively holding. It all comes down to what is known as the inner vision mode, which is a perspective of ordinary mental awareness. As previously said, this is the part of oneself that is insensitive to spiritual worlds. To view auras and otherworldly creatures, this cognitive model of vision must be turned off.

As a result, there is one key that you become aware of the fact of seeing rather than focusing on the contents of the image. Typically, you will examine the image with the vision to determine if the material is round, rectangular, yellow, ugly, lovely, and so on. However, you are now acting differently from a non-mental standpoint.

You lose faith in the picture's elements. Rather, you know that it is evident. You quit trying to see and understand. You shift your attention from the source of awareness to the apparent process. You begin to focus on the motion of the sight, the actuality of seeing, rather than the item itself.

This first interaction degree is composed of two sections that must be performed simultaneously in front of a buddy or a mirror: As little as possible, total stillness with a narrow eye concentration, oblivious to the fact that one sees rather than looks.

Length of eye contact session: Begin with 5 minutes. Increase the time gradually to 15 minutes or more.

When Seeing Is a Problem

In this book, we will discuss three types of vision, the first of which is the immovability of the eye. Please keep the following considerations in mind if you find it difficult to return to see it:

- The understanding of visuality must be incorrect. A barely perceptible sensation is enough to reveal the procedure.
- If you cannot attain a basic understanding of the reality of seeing, then temporarily disregard it and proceed as before.
- Recognize that you are looking at an image. Ignore your companion or the mirror, as well as any photographic information.
- Instead of gazing at the snapshot, try to see it.

- Follow the cycle by replacing sight with feeling. instead of gazing at it.
- Things will become clear as you go.
- To avoid certain eye tests, close your eyes.
- Place your hands together for a few seconds. Put your hands on the closed eyes that are covering your face so that they are not kept away from the flesh. Fire from your hands should permeate your eyeballs. Rest here for a while and enjoy the rejuvenating impact.
- Throughout this time, you will experience memorable inner-light interactions.
- Tap your thumbs, then open your eyes. Then you and your pal talk about it.
- Then start again. Close your eyes for three minutes to reconnect. Then, once again, close your eyes and maintain eye contact.

Suggestions and Tricks

What happens when you attain perfect motionlessness and your energy dissipates? Among other things, the link between the astral body and the bodily condition is weakened.

The vibration layer is the astral body. You may feel astral while hearing the vibration. The astral presence is no longer locked in the conscious mind after you reach ultimate quiet, which is more than just a lack of motion. Regardless of awareness, it is somewhat emancipated and more easily available for other activities. There will also be a strong tremor throughout.

Should I Blink or Should I Not Blink?

All of this is to say that you should not be afraid but rather rejoice when your eyes swell and tears flow from them. According to Hatha's ancient knowledge, it relieves eye tension and cures numerous diseases. Use common sense, but gradually increase length and avoid pushing motion. There is no spiritual intent in causing oneself suffering.

Suggestions and Tricks

As is customary, there are instances when working with energy makes it simple and easy to remain blind for lengthy periods of time. It's as if there's a deadly smoke cloud in front of your eyes at times, and you can't stop blinking every two seconds.

The safest technique is to accept the colorful and fluctuating dynamics of energy and keep practicing without attaching too much emphasis to those changes. A handful of increasing experiences with eye contact. Sharp shapes are being softened in the picture.

Don't resist making the image even blurry. Before you may comprehend nonphysical pictures, you must first surrender your outward image. As a result, let the true image gets muddled and obscured. Even if it serves no purpose, go with the flow. The perception may be studied afterward. This will never happen if you worry about it for as long as you do.

Both physical and nonphysical representations would be possible at different stages of development. However, you must first eliminate the tight edges and allow the image to diffuse until the ethereal hues and shadows are visible.

It's a good indicator if the person in front of you is taller than the man. It signifies you've switched from the apparent world to the subtle realm. As soon as you reach the comprehension of the astral plane, the distances become relatively clear. It is fairly uncommon for the person sitting in front of you to seem distant. If this is the case, you know that what you see is not of this world.

Light does not originate from the sun or other sources, such as candles in the astral worlds. Items and other entities may be observed due to their brightness. Their light is unleashed. They are usually lighted in a semi-dark setting.

However, it should be understood that astral colors vary greatly from actual hues. As a result, the lack of similarities in our material surroundings makes it practically hard to identify them precisely. A significant distinction is that a color combination always seems ethereal. However, unlike what is observed in the physical world, the many components of an astral hue do not merge.

When two colors merge, everything fades, and an intermediary shadow forms in the Real World. Green is created by combining blue and yellow. The yellow and blue have vanished, and the green has emerged. Colors in the astral realm are often hundreds of little, bright dots. Glossy blue dots, yellow dots, and green dots, for example, are tightly interwoven together in the hues we emphasized. In certain cases, ethereal hues are completely uniform.

Their range and remarkable grace extend well beyond what is seen in the corporeal world.

Because of the distinction between ethereal and exterior hues, it is typically unnecessary to search for an aura of yellow, blue, or green. As a result, while reading some publications that point out that green in one spectrum, blue in another, and so on, one must be cautious. It is common to oversimplify unnecessary statements.

The space where you exercise is dark, and the temperature of the light fluctuates. Mystics referred to the atmosphere as astral light. It is a basic hue that penetrates the astral plane, and when you concentrate on your thoughts, it is no different from the black light you perceive. It is also known as 'astral darkness,' since it seems to be a semi-blackness that is obviously fainter than visible light but of a different kind than the darkness of our evenings. The genuine darkness has no light. The astral anonymity shows through, thus the Masonic term "visible anonymity."

When you make eye contact and the surrounding area dims instantaneously, even in the middle of the day, this indicates that you can see the Astral Light. You go from your physical world experience to your astral space experience. Quite often, it will be accompanied by a specific color vision: They will look to you, as shown in the previous paragraphs.

Astral space is not singular nor homogenous. As you develop in meditation and travel, you learn to navigate through astral regions. One of the guidelines that help you find your path is the brightness of the colors and the basic shade of astral light, which varies based on the place you sleep. Some areas of the room have a milky tint, while others are deeper, nearly black, or even bright blue as if they are under the sea. These hue alterations may also be seen before entering the overall stage of your journey.

The amazing thing is that once your thinking has matured, you can look at all of these levels at the same time. At some point throughout the opening process, you may also incorporate the tangible world in your vision. The grandeur of the earth is so stunning with this explosion of colors that it frees the mind. At times, beauty is at the pinnacle of what is bearable. Life is a never-ending marvel and a lot of pleasure.

Instead of your friend's appearance, a new one emerges. It is one of the most common situations in which you practice your eye contact strategies: Your friend's face is missing, but another face is visible. If you practice alone in front of a mirror, your own face vanishes and is replaced by another. These expressions basically represent four options:

- A spirit advisor
- A previous existence
- A secondary personality
- A person or thing

CHAPTER 5

THE BENEFITS OF SEEING W THE APPLICATION OF DARKNESS

We've been conditioned to reach for the light switch or a flashlight whenever we need to find our way in the dark. You can get along without light in a variety of situations.

At the very least, imagine you're a cat. Switch to cat mode. Rely on the instinct you know you have. Also, be extremely aware of your gaze.

At night, there is a cluster of energy surrounding various kinds of things, some of which are highly visible. It is one of those senses that most people miss, and it is not because they believe it is difficult or sophisticated. If you walk a dirt route in the countryside at night, you may notice that the road shines when seen through the third eye. It's a good idea to attempt to find your way without artificial light. You may also rediscover your apartment at night or in the middle of the day.

If at all feasible, use candles instead of electric lighting; more candles and fuel lamps, less electricity. In the natural light of candles, you have much better access to auras.

For obvious reasons, electric lights are not associated with the perceptual opening. To humans, the light from a light bulb seems to be continuous.

However, this is not the case. Electric lights operate on 50-hertz alternating current. It signifies that the light activates and deactivates several times each second. The process is rapid enough to fool your perception, yet this frequency is recorded subconsciously. It has caused cerebral activity.

Consider turning on and off an electric light every half second to see the light pulsing. What is the end result? Very heartbreaking!

To protect yourself, you may need to shut your eyes or build a mental structure, such as a screen. This implies that you must shield your eyes to some degree.

When you begin to utilize your eyes, you will notice that the electrical light switches on and off multiple times each second. It's difficult in the brain. To protect you, something deep inside must be turned off.

The opening is, of course, the overall direction of vision. We spoke about how the mind's desire to withdraw is one of the most difficult impediments to seeing. For example, you see an aura and your mind becomes shocked, afraid, or intrigued. This mental response results in an abrupt closure. In a fraction of a second, your perception is gone, and you must begin to reopen it. Electric light causes a comparable shutting action at a low unconscious level.

However, I am not in support of turning off all of your home's electric lights! But make no mistake about it! When reading or writing, for example, use electric light. Little light fatigues your eyes, making it difficult to focus.

The argument is that using candles while practicing eye contact or other visualization methods is considerably superior. Furthermore, there are numerous situations in which we use electric lights because of habit rather than desire, such as dining or conversing with a friend. So, we may take use of such occasions to liberate our minds and practice visualization skills. This is one of the spiritual practice's success secrets: utilize your everyday activities to adopt processes more and more. Integrate your mind-opening practice with easy acts.

However, electric lighting must become a worry in the long run. It would be a benefit for mankind if someone could produce some type of artificial light that would soften our subconscious perception.

When attempting to see an aura, you will obtain much better results if the item or person is black and white or painted in a very light color. If you actually want to see, remodel the walls of the rooms where you spend most of your time. Certain white hues and wall representations have a magical effect: when someone stands in front of them, halos of light appear.

The Shawl in White

When practicing eye contact methods with the same acquaintance on a daily basis, wearing a white shawl that covers your garments might be beneficial. It makes seeing auras easier and attracts all types of positive energies. Viewing becomes more difficult while wearing black or dark clothing. Wear a white scarf while practicing alone or in front of the mirror. The shawl may be made from cotton, silk, or linen. However, there are no synthetic fibers. Wear it whenever you meditate to help you concentrate your energy. Every time you put on the shawl, your energy is energized and you feel happy. Allow no one else to use the shawl or all your hard work will be undone in a matter of minutes.

I recommend a shawl since it is simple to make: There is no sewing required; just a pair of scissors required!

However, a dress may be created (a size of 1 meter by two and perhaps 2.5 is generally adequate). Even though the knowledge was forgotten, monks' robes were originally meant to aid in the concentration and protection of energy. Perhaps it is time to create a new generation of energy apparel.

Aura Observation Techniques for Beginners

The simplest approach to get an aura or contact someone's guides is to follow the steps below:

- You may sit with an eye contact distance of roughly 90 cm between you or with greater room surrounding you, like in a typical chat. Better still: Begin your eye contact in a comfortable and informal setting, then repeat your exercise to compare your results.

- Breathing via throat friction. Close your eyes for a minute or two. Connect with space in the eye via a brief third eye meditation, as previously stated.

- The friction will then dissipate, and your eyes will open. It entails staring at the person whose aura you wish to read and doing the three-step visionary technique mentioned above, 1 or 2 millimeters above the head.

- Maintain a clear and steady gaze. Blink as little as possible.

- There are no details in the image. Be conscious of what you are seeing. If you continue to perceive a mystery, just feel the picture rather than look at it.

- Feel the other person in your heart at the core of your chest.

- Stay completely motionless in this three-process immersion.

- After a few minutes, begin the throat friction. Link the picture to the friction.

- When you're through, rub your hands together. Focus your attention on your palms. Allow your gaze to go to the warmth inside.

Tips

- Once you've linked the halos to the throat friction, you'll be amazed by the dramatic improvement in your perception of halos. It demonstrates the magnifying impact of friction.

- The technique is to tune the spiritual entities over the individual's mind and have the person read for you to create an aura of reading. Set your sight to on and monitor your sight.

Where Should You Specifically Look During Eye Contact?

The secret is hidden because it is evident. However, the issue remains: Where do you look? Especially before your perception shifts to space at the beginning of the exercise. You certainly can.

- Examine your partner's eyes.
- Examine one of his eyes.
- Try to gaze at yourself without touching the physical portion of your spouse.

Experiment with the many possibilities, moving from one to the next.

The actual image will vanish after a time, so what you pick isn't really important. When you concentrate on the eyes of the person in front of you, everything blurs but your eyes stay clear, or your face changes but your eyes remain the same.

Whatever choice you choose, both individuals like to do the same thing at the same time.

Remember that focusing between your eyes does not imply converging your eyeballs as if you were attempting to glance around. It simply implies that your third eye should be maintained open.

Occasionally, the channel will be released.
A few channel releases are useful from time to time when working on these clear-sighted tactics. This activates your whole etheric body, strengthening the etheric layer of your third eye; do not be afraid to use channel releases if your progress seems to be stalled.

Working on Auras Here are a few ideas to help you improve your aura awareness.
Begin with a hyperlink: Closing your eyes, inhaling with throat friction, and increasing the brow vibration. Then relax and become aware of the black space for 2 minutes.

Start the three-vision procedure by opening your eyes:

1. The eye's attention in the absence of motion
2. The sensation of the eye
3. The sensation of the heart

The aim is to remain extremely still inside and be absorbed by that threefold process, to ask your buddy before you say or think about various topics to see if there is any change in your aura as a consequence. You may position yourself an inch above or between your brows as desired. Of course, avoid peering too closely. Otherwise, you won't see anything.

For about a minute, have your acquaintance repeat the phrase "No, No, No..."

It should be a No with meaning, a No that means No. Feel the quality of light surrounding him at this moment.

Ask your acquaintance to repeat "Yes, Yes, Yes..." for a minute on purpose. Feel the light and evaluate the quality of the energy.

Repeat with "No" once or twice, then "Yes" once or twice. Rep the technique, but this time your buddy should be conscious in his eye and around his belly while saying no. Ask your yes-saying friend:

- For one or two minutes, be completely present in your heart.
- Consider death for a moment; then ask your companion to be calm.

Tips

You may repeat the activity, but this time ask your buddy to remember:

- A well-liked individual
- The person he or she dislikes
- Someone who has passed away

Other approaches to investigating these activities will come to mind. When you read the chapter on ley lines, you may see your friend's aura while he or she sits:

- On a poisonous crossing of the earth's borders, knowingly.
- Inadvertently crossing a dangerous line on the earth's surface.
- On energy well.

Aura Analysis

It's also fun to have your buddy hold different things and chemicals and see how the aura changes as a result. (If it's extremely excellent, as soon as the person steps on it, the effect on the aura is immediate and noticeable.) Request that your buddy do the task. You may place the item in front of your heart and then other areas of your body to check if the aura changes.

Here Are Some Suggestions Here

- A vessel made of copper.
- A large wooden handle, but no tool (a thermometer tip).
- A variety of food cans in metal cups.
- Frozen meal packets.
- Platters with various meals.
- Try everything--ordinary and extraordinary-- herbs, medications, medicines, and homeopathic remedies.

Tips

The practice is known as muscle testing,' and it is based on the premise that a muscle's strength increases when you think about something correctly or hold a nice material. On the contrary, if you use the incorrect cure or think about anything that is false or harmful to you, your muscular strength should decrease.

Some patients, for example, are instructed to hold bottles in front of their hearts with their left hand while extending their right arm horizontally. The individual pushes his hand down to test the strength of his shoulder muscle.

The approach has limits, and making it a universal way of knowing does not seem realistic. It is remarkable, however, because muscular resistance varies greatly depending on what the guy believes or believes.

while you start sensing auras while you think about various things or have different drugs, you will notice that there are distinct distinctions in a person's energy. You don't even have to "see" aura to detect it; you only have to feel it.

Vata, Pitta, and Kapha

Ayurveda, or Indian traditional medicine, recognizes three principles in the body:

- Vata, wind-fire and heat.
- Kapha, water and land, and inertia force.

Ayurvedic diagnosis is based on the prevailing principle of these three (known as the three doshas) in a patient. Patients are classed as' Vata,' or' Pitta,' or' Kapha,' or'

Vata-Pitta,' or' Pitta,' or' Kapha-Vata,' and so on if the two doshas are hyperactive.

We had a process (it was actually a game) to pulse the patients and examine their aura. Before he offered his diagnosis, I would write mine in a book. Then we'd compare them. The doctor was in excellent health and saw up to 100 people every day. This is not uncommon in India. This was a good sample to illustrate how often we agreed.

And we had the same diagnosis in more than 90% of the instances. Don't assume you need to do it on an expert level right now. You don't need to be able to see auras to feel them. Sit at a busy road café and see people walking about in the tripartite process of viewing. Determine if you are a 'Vata' or a 'Pita,' for example.
Give the same item to a buddy so you may compare your results. You'll be surprised at how frequently you agree. Prepare to make eye contact with your pal.

Communication without using words
Plug your ears and do the triple vision exercise.
Your buddy then repeats five words to himself. Every phrase is repeated three times. When the kid starts a new statement, he or she indicates the appropriate

finger number (phrase 1, phrase 2). Your objective is to identify the statements that include solely misleading references to auras.

Rep the exercise without your ears blocked this time. To determine whether the assertion is untrue, try depending just on the aura rather than what you hear.

Tips

An eye-opening discovery is that sometimes not listening and focusing on the aura is more effective than examining the message's substance.

Do not be afraid to cheat and contribute to the sport with more than one incorrect statement!

Take a look at these samples to understand more about sight. Western esoteric, such as Rudolf Steiner, discussed how individuals in the distant past had radically different ways of experiencing warmth. Some kind of saggy organ was perched on their skulls. The region now corresponds to the fontanelle on top of the child's head, a soft membrane between the two parietal bones. If we go back a long, long time in nature's memory vault, we may learn that Earth was full of volcanoes and places with hot gas and plasmas. To prevent being roasted alive, people must have a sense of direction. The baggy thing on top of their heads served as a rudimentary organ of warmth.

What happened with evolution? The saggy half was within our heads and was gradually reintegrated into our pineal gland. And our experience of warmth is now distributed throughout the body rather than being restricted to a single organ. We may therefore track the evolution of a sensory function across time. It is dependent on and restricted to one organ before spreading slowly across the body. We no longer sense warmth in a specific organ, but rather across the body. Steiner predicted that all of our current senses will evolve in a similar way, allowing humans to smell, see, hear, and taste. And not just via a single organ, but throughout their whole body. It's as though the nearby organ gives us a lesson, and when the lesson is through, we no longer need it.

Because the experience of warmth is considerably older and hence more interwoven with our being, independent of any object, we can better comprehend what it is. It is possible to perceive the genuine warmth quality. Let us use this as an analogy to get further knowledge.

It may be tough to establish a sensation of seeing in the beginning, regardless of the picture. It is seeing a tree and seeing the light that allows us to sense what it is. However, nude seeing may not be as obvious.

The sensation of warmth is used to heat picture views. We cannot comprehend what is common by referring to ideas such as "heat as a burning fire," "heated as the sun," or "heated as a stove." We can only go to the heat and feel warmth, regardless of the source of heat. It must be developed in order to discern between visions. It is of comparable quality.

In other words, perception requires three components:

- A perceptive individual.
- An item that will be perceived.
- Perception procedures.

This extends to all bodily sensations, including hearing and smell, and not only seeing auras.

The first and third aspects, the perceiver's consciousness and the awareness process, have been lost in most people's everyday lives. For example, when you look at a tree, you identify it intellectually, but you don't know who sees it or how it is interpreted. The seen thing is absorbed. Being able to see implies being aware of the perceiving process.

In this work, we genuinely want to discover ourselves; we don't just utilize procedures to attain perception. Perception is used to attain the Self.

When you have two oranges and a basket full of cherries, the oranges may easily conceal the cherry. When you take the two oranges out of the basket, the cherry stands out. One orange represents a perception object, the other the perception process, and the cherry represents the perceiver's self-awareness. By separating eyes from perceived things, you obtain a discerning experience similar to taking the two oranges from the basket. As a result, as you become conscious of seeing, you may experience such powerful flashes of inner awakening--sudden inner explosions that unveil your Self.

Your insights will progressively deepen as you continue to practice the tripartite visionary process. At first, it looks dim. However, with experience, it becomes more palpable, as distinct and obvious as the feeling of warmth. The visions might also be likened to a muscle that hasn't been utilized in a long time. Muscle reactivation will most likely be gradual at first: It doesn't feel, you don't know if it contracts or not, and it's quite feeble. When you have completed your task, it is plain and evident to activate your visions when you contract your biceps. In truth, subtle bodybuilding is part of the inner alchemy process, not physical bodybuilding.

There is now a paradox: ignore everything since the visual content is irrelevant to you. In brief, you take one of the two oranges from the basket. The perceptual object has been eliminated. The second orange (seeing, the perceptual process) then becomes self-evident. However, once your viewpoint has evolved, you behave differently.

It makes no difference whether the object of perception is directly opposite you, on the other side of the globe, or even on the other side of the galaxy. It makes no difference whether the object of awareness is on this side of the lexical world or not, and something strange often occurs: You may choose to shut your eyes to view something better right in front of you.

The issue then becomes, "How can you become completely disinterested in the object if you view it with visuals?"

The key to this contradiction is that once you reach that point, you no longer look at the item with your thoughts. The mind is quiet, and you perceive from a deeper and more accurate level.

That's why the first piece of advice is to not gaze at the thing or get very interested in it. Because you have been trained to function only using your mind, your mind will be activated if you do not. When you are interested in something, your mind will instinctively want to understand it.

To enable the vision process to develop, it is better to avoid thinking about the item at all.

Often, you will have an intriguing encounter from the start. You will start to notice an aura, another face, or a spiritual creature. Then it appears and vanishes. What is the explanation behind this? Because you responded to your thoughts. You've suddenly been fascinated, terrified, or anything else; in other words, you've seized the mind. You take another glance from your head. It is natural for you to lose perception as a result of nature's blindness of the usual mind. When you start the perception process, it will continue until you respond and then end when your mind first understands. Your ability to respond is constantly constrained by the boundaries of your perception.

What are you looking for?

Some think that one of your eyes corresponds to your deeper and genuine Self, while the other represents your superficial demeanor. Let us not say which eye since our attitude is to believe nothing other than to grasp what is meant to happen to us. The following exercise is intended to assist you in determining if there are any discrepancies in what each eye can see. Sit down and prepare yourself for eye contact.

Remember, if you can't touch your hand to another person's face, you're too far away. Straighten up your back.

Practice a brief reconnection into your eye, then open your eyes and begin staring at the other person's right eye (this exercise may also be done by yourself using a mirror). Your friend's right eye is in focus, and your friend's right eye is in focus. To avoid any misunderstanding, I propose that you raise your right hand at the start of the exercise to guarantee that you both stare at the correct eye.

Then, with the unmoving focus between your brows, the awareness of seeing, and the sense of the heart, begin the process of three visions.

Follow the practice for around 5 minutes. Then, for a little pause, shut your eyes and warm your eyelids with your palms as indicated earlier.

To prevent misunderstanding, open your eyes and show each other with your left hand. Begin by glancing at each other's left eye and repeat for a few minutes. Close your eyes, cup your hands, and warm your heart.

Make an Exchange with a Friend Your Thoughts

After trying this practice on hundreds of individuals, I don't believe a word of the presumption that one of your eyes relates to the Higher Self and the other to the Lower Self. It's still amazing to see how different someone might seem depending on which eye you look at.

It's a true feeling to consider how different someone appears.

Of course, each eye connects to a separate subpersonality, and there is more than one eye-related subpersonality. It's important recalling that the term "person" comes from the Etruscan word verse, which means "mask."

Here's a great yes/yes strategy. What, in fact, hinders you from becoming a visionary? Of course, must put the methods into action. You must engage in subtle bodybuilding. But your sensitive vision organ must function from time to time; you may have a one-second flash, a precious little instant in which you see! And it's gone, and it might take months for such a flash to happen.

What happens next? Barriers, mental screens, lax mental awareness, self-protective routines, and dense circumstances like a vice are all preventing you from moving forward.

This approach is intended to assist you in breaking down spiritual barriers. It needs someone to sit with you and practice; you cannot do it alone in front of a mirror.

- Place your feet squarely in front of each other. If you can't touch your face with the palm of your hand, you're too far away.

- Reassemble your eye by closing your eyes. Consider the throat friction. Make the vibration of the eye. Place it in a dark place for 2 minutes.

- Please open your eyes. Implement the three-fold vision process: focus in the eye, see with the heart, and feel with the heart. Try to incorporate the other into your heart.

- When you're ready, one of them says, "Yes." And the other adds, when you're ready, say "yes."

This is a hrt-centered practice. You couldn't get away with it. The other person will sense it right away, and it will not happen if you put up any barriers or restrictions. You must utter a "yes" that really means "yes," and give it greater significance and openness. Yes, should come from the heart. You must continue to work on each other's deepening until the other person has complete acceptance. Then proceed. Accept the approval of the whole world by the individual in front of you.

Continue to practice for as long as you like. Then, for two or three minutes, cover your closed eyes with your hands and allow the warmth of your eyes to reach your heart.

You've been astounded by how many individuals say "yes" when, in reality, they mean "no." Or they immediately say 'yes' after 'yes'.

Put yourself through this exercise, and you won't be able to talk for a few minutes. The word seemed to come from a distance.

This will help you to really feel your own truth.
There is no time restriction on how long the practice may go.

CHAPTER 6

PRACTICES FOR THE ETHERIC BODY

Let us now proceed with the channel release strategies. We go to the following level after becoming more conscious of the vibration and its circulation: The consciousness of the complete energy body, also known as the etheric layer.

This chapter's exercises should not be done at the start of a session. Warm up your etheric body with some channel release exercises.

In a meditation pose, the whole etheric layer settles down with your back straight. Keep your eyes closed at all times.

Rub your hands together and remain stationary for a few seconds with your palms up. Recognize the vibration in your hands and eyes. Use throat friction to amplify the vibration and link the eyes and hands.

Several Meridians Channel Release should be implemented.

Then, be conscious of the vibration in all of the lines you worked on previously: All of the meridians are conscious at the same moment.

All of the friction should be connected to your eye.Then become aware of the full vibratory layer – everything that vibrates inside and around your body. Allow your perception to be completely engulfed by the vibration.

When you sense just the vibration surrounding your body and nothing else, it implies you have totally transferred your awareness from the physical to the etheric body. The ether of life pervades the whole etheric layer's awareness.

Maintain your immobility while feeling your whole body vibrate.

Then attempt to figure out where the life force is in this frequency. What keeps your body going? What? Adjust the life principle.

Tips

- Although the whole etheric body is related to life's vigor, one of its levels is more life-specific: the ether of life. Occultists have traditionally identified four strata in the etheric body.

- They are the ether of life, the ether of chemicals, and the ether of light and warmth. The term "layer" might be misleading since the four ethers are not piled up like cake layers. Rather, they permeate each other in the same way that water penetrates a sponge.

- There are two groupings of four letters: two lower and two higher. The lower ethers are life and chemical ether, whereas the upper ethers are light and warmth. The two upper ethers are now underdeveloped and must be developed in the majority of humans.

- The most precious energy, in reality, is a living force. No one living entity could ever create our modern civilization's laboratory! Connecting particularly to life ether is a really unique experience. The taste of awareness linked with it is difficult to put into words.

- The ether of life seems to be a universal principle that is not restricted to the physical body. If you try to trace the origins of your awareness, you will end yourself in strange places. The others are followed by a powerful vision and travel technology.

- Try this technique at different times of the day, such as in the morning and evening, to see if there is any change in your energy in life. Also, if you're fatigued, have a look at it.

- Although attempting to differentiate these four levels right now would be quite premature, it is useful to recall the etheric' s fourfold divide. It will assist you in distinguishing them from your perspective.

- It's a fascinating reality that we view what our minds can admit as more easily perceived. The sense that we have no pattern of explanation, particularly when it is weak, is more likely to be overlooked than in the start.

- An intriguing anthropological remark on the subject: Several movies depict some South American peoples living in the bush, cut off from industrial and civilizational items. One video shows a square revolving on itself, much like an empty window frame. These folks, who dwell in a non-square environment, are unable to notice the square rotating. You just see moving lines. There are no squares in the mental backdrop of the rotation of the empty window framework.

- Something like that tends to happen rather often when individuals are open. Many impressions are absent as a result of a lack of background that allows them to integrate. They just do not notice anything that enters their perceptual region since they cannot attach to any pattern of knowledge. A fundamental understanding of the geography of the non-physical worlds and certain basic astral occurrences may therefore aid in perception.

Explore diverse etheric properties and become aware of your whole etheric layer. Stay still and attempt to detect different properties in the ether.

Then, investigate other sections of the body and compare the vibratory variations between them. For example, if you have a sensation of the life ether, check to see whether it is evenly distributed throughout your body.

First, compare the extremities and trunk.
What is the difference between limb and trunk vibration? How do the trunk and the head stack up? What is the difference between vibration on the head and vibration on the trunk?

Determine the portion of the body after the part of the body. Is the vibration stronger in some of them?

How does the quality of the vibration differ from organ to organ?Do particular organs or bodily parts make you feel overwhelmed by life? Are other individuals experiencing the same way?

Tips

If you have a physical ailment, you must indicate the relevant area of practice.

For example, one to two hours after a substantial lunch, it may be advisable to repeat this technique under different conditions.

Make yourself aware of the full layer of vibration. Experimenting with limits

How far does your vibration extend beyond the confines of your physical body?

Is your physical body's vibration similar to that of the outside world? What is the quality difference between the inner and outer vibration?

Continue to study the vibrations that exist outside of your body's boundaries. Is there anything that stands out? Does your vibration interact with the items around you?

Explore the etheric circulations and become aware of the full layer of vibration. Assume you're in charge of acupuncture reinvention. In the vibration layer, look for circulations. Look for anything that makes you feel like the vibration is flowing through your body.

Start with your whole body. Keep an eye out for the overall circulation of the energy body.Is one more intense than another? Is there a distinction between huge and small?

Can you distinguish qualitative distinctions between various flows? Do you become hot and cold for some of them? Do some have a comparable sense to one of the four elements (fire, water, air, or land)?

Partially explored areas include the head, neck, thighs, arms, thighs, abdomen above and below the navel; legs, abdomen below the navel. Then return to the sense of the vibration over the whole etheric body. Repeat the procedure a few times.

Outside Your Body Etheric Vibration

This is best done in a natural setting, such as a forest. A backyard with a little grass and one or two trees, on the other hand, is adequate. There will also be potted plants and a cat!

Do a brief third-eye meditation and then link with the complete vibration layer inside you. Feel the life-power vibration in your body. At the same moment, the vibration between the brows is completely conscious.

Then, choose a tree or plant and attempt to analyze its vibration. Don't touch the plant; just tune it out. Continue to analyze the plant's vibration quality for many minutes.

How far is the plant's vibration going beyond its physical limits? When you tune into the vibration of the plant, can you notice any circulation? Then, a few millimeters away from the plant, position your flat hands without touching them. The vibration of the plant must be felt, and its qualities must be investigated.

Then, from a distance, listen in to another plant. Repeat the procedure, but this time compare the quality of the plant's vibration to the quality of the prior vibration.

Then shut your hands and go through their vibration again.

Repeat with other plants. Then attempt to adjust to the creatures and learn about their vibration quality.

Tips

- Nature is transformed into an intriguing area by this method. Going one step further makes friendship with nature a reality.

- The idea that once you can feel something in yourself, you can feel it outside of yourself is a shocking but essential reality. The more acquainted you get, for example, the simpler it is to sense the vibration within your body. It is critical to recognize not just the etheric layer, but also the complete gamut of subtle sensations. This statement is correct.

- When you sense certain things outside of yourself, you often get to perceive them within. When you apply your awareness to the outside world, certain "clicks" happen that make you realize you had entirely neglected a layer inside yourself.

- The environment becomes a mirror in which new forms of oneself might be found, hence the idea of 'clearing vision' or ego vision.

- When doing these exercises, remember to keep your eyes focused: Keep the vibrations between your brows fully conscious—anything you wish to touch from between the eyes.

- It is fairly uncommon for individuals to forget and attempt to accomplish anything "from their heads" from their regular thoughts. However, if you tell them to return to the eye and attempt to sense it, they will come into touch with the object's vibration right away.

- When you adapt to certain streams and lakes, they have a very rich vibratory character and convey tremendous soul energy. The ocean also does this. Spending time in nature can help you increase your awareness. Tuning with nature's forces delivers huge realizations in addition to increasing your vibrational experience.

Meals with Vibration

As your experience of the vibration grows more familiar, it is crucial to incorporate it into your regular routines. This provides an additional layer to your spectrum of aware experiences.

Experiment with vibration during meals, for example. Feel it both before and during meals. Without vision, the food you eat is like a poison to your spirit. Feeling the vibration offers you a whole new perspective on the worth of specific meals. Some beautiful foods suddenly seem to be terrible. Some of them are just plain fascinating.

Compare the vibration of frozen food, canned food, and microwave-cooked food... Can you tell the difference between organic and non-organic fruits and vegetables? Use your perspective while shopping. Some veggies will virtually spring into your hands.

Try to feel the vibration in the organ as it digests the first portion of the digestion down the heart behind the left ribcage; it's also extremely instructive to tune in to your stomach during digestion. You discover that different foods produce quite diverse vibrational kinds.

The Vibration in the Bath

You should be submerged not only in your shoulders but also in the back of your head and ears. It is a nice posture to recline in the water with your legs crossed as if you were sitting cross-legged. You then glide smoothly and harmoniously with your trunk and head. Keep your arms at your sides rather than your chest on your belly.

If you are familiar with Hatha-yoga, you may also attempt to soak the fish in many Sana.

However, it is sufficient to display the location at the start of this section. You need to be as comfortable as possible for as long as possible, so pick an easy position.

Place yourself in your bath and relax for a while.

Create the eye vibration and become aware of your full etheric vibration. Respire to relieve throat friction. The friction is amplified when your ears are submerged in water. The water's vibration then becomes aware. Forget about your body and focus only on the water. Get out and experience the water's vibration. You will discover that not all water has the same properties. The water vibration of the same bath might vary dramatically from day to day.

After a time, you should be able to sense the interplay between the water vibration and your own vibration. What effect does the former have on the latter?

Tips

- The physical body is related to the Earth's element, the astral body's air element, the Ego's fire element, and the etheric body's water element. It is thus quite suitable to explore your etheric depth on the water. Do not be afraid to repeat all of the procedures in this chapter during your bath to uncover your etheric characteristics, circulation, and restrictions.

- Never pass up a chance to tune into vibration when in the water. You'll be astonished at how refreshed you feel after having a bath with this approach. Bathwater will also reveal any changes in your vibrational quality (both in the water and in yourself) caused by essential oils and other (natural) things. Because essential oils are subtle, you may benefit from them by adjusting their energy.

- In a bath, crush a little ginger and heat for 15 minutes to get a fine juice. Add the liquid after squeezing the bathwater. The skin has an amazing cleaning effect.

- Swimming in lakes, rivers, waterfalls, or the ocean with that new sensation of water will be exciting. However, it will not entice you to visit public swimming pools, which might amass a lot of unpleasant vibrations.

Excretion of Etheric

While completely conscious of the vibrations throughout your body, you seek energies inside you that may be ambiguous or bad. For one minute, investigate and sensitize undesired vibrations.

Negative vibrations should be removed from the water vibration. Push out your etheric layer of undesired vibrations with extended, deliberate exhalations and powerful throat frictions. One of the keys of etheric excretion is as follows: It works best when you're about to expire.

As a result, it works even better when you 'consciously' exhale by forcing yourself to expel the breath rather than automatically. For this goal of elimination, make friction when exhaling rather than inhaling. And the friction should be much greater than normal. Don't linger in the bath for too long after you've finished excreting.

Tips

Try this approach if you have a headache. When adopted early on, it often produces outstanding benefits at the beginning of a crisis. The procedures described in this Chapter bring up new possibilities for the growing hydrotherapy field.

Remove the water. When a large number of individuals use the same bath, you must be cautious. part individuals are nervous when they pull the plug and let the water run while in the restroom, as though part of their own power has been wasted. (Hindu Gurus highlighted the importance of their own restroom.) Test yourself to see whether you're accomplishing anything.

Loo Practice

I can never emphasize enough the importance of 'etheric excretion,' which has largely been forgotten by people. Farsighted people can see this well. Apart from a few drainage procedures in homeopathy, acupuncture, and herbalism, both conventional and alternative therapies are presently underutilized. None of them are very efficient when compared to the capacity to excrete through conscious etheric layer waking.

The more you use your etheric excretion talent, the more tangible it becomes. Certain etheric frequencies will exit your etheric body as plainly as the stools you feel leave your physical body.

Some etheric excretions may occur in the absence of physical ones. All physical excretions, however, should be regarded to be accompanied by etheric excretions.

Ethnic excretions are nothing like that because of what homeopaths term the population's innate psoric miasm. Keep an eye on your vibration layer when your pee or feces pass through. Apply oneself in conjunction with physical matter to transmit negative etheric vibrations. The strength of the outcomes and the overall sense of well-being created will astound you.

Unexpectedly powerful energy movements occur during urine and in lower volumes when feces pass through, however, they normally go undetected.

Introducing to the Earth

As your capacity to excrete etheric substances grows, you will be able to carry releases not just into the water but also into the soil. Remove your shoes, place your socks on the ground, and place your soles on the ground.

Keep your eyes shut. Engage in throat friction and feel the vibration throughout your eye and body. Then let go of your body and feel the earth's vibration. After 1 or 2 minutes, begin the excretion of etheric vibrations in the ground. Exhale deeply with powerful, friction-intensive exhalations. Put unwanted vibrations into the soil when the breath leaves your lips.

On Earth, they are not dangerous vibrations. They are composted and turned into new natural powers. This may also help with the discharge of colds or tension.

Tips

As with anything strong, this approach should be used with caution. Otherwise, your energy reserves may be drained.

Hugging Trees

Here's another practice related to etheric discharge. The next time you tune in, you're in a forest, and you choose a huge tree with which you feel very close. Make as much touch with the surface as possible: Hold the trunk with your arms and press your chest, belly, and legs against it.

Remove any unwanted vibrations from the tree. Just like you, excrete them into the bathwater. Give it to the tree as a present. When you're finished, thank the tree.

Tips

To begin, consider releasing bad energy into water or the soil. Keep trees for finer vibes or energies that you can't get rid of any other way. In any case, it doesn't inherently harm the tree; it's something useful to provide. Although the frequency linked with a low mood or the beginning of the flu may seem bad to you, it is a highly advanced, intelligent energy for the tree. When you apply your awareness, you might find plants that crave what you are attempting to erase from yourself.

This method has the potential to be quite effective. However, you have at least 10 to 15 minutes to remain against the tree, if feasible. You must give the tree enough time to accept what you are attempting to impart.

Crying

Shedding tears may help you shed a lot of unnecessary emotional strain and energy, especially if you use your new etheric excretion potential. Put whatever you wish to get rid of in tears.

Crying is a vital skill to have on the road to self-transformation (if feasible, at will!). It allows you to deeply cleanse your heart. If you are the sort of person who can never weep, I recommend that you work hard to reclaim that capacity. If, on the other hand, you are the kind of person who cries a little too much, it is possible that by crying more, you will not have to weep as much since the aim is to raise quality while decreasing quantity.

Use any tactic, from peeling onions to more complicated dramatic art skills.

Sweeping the Citrus Mother was also a renowned Occultist of the twentieth century, in addition to being in charge of the Sri Aurobindo Ashram in Pondicherry for many years. She recalled working with Mrs. King, an outstanding mental lady. Mrs. King was capable of placing a grapefruit on her chest while she reclined and sucked in her energies.

After a time, the grapefruit had lost all of its vitality. Even physically, the fruit seemed withered. Can you do the same with grapefruit or orange?

Lying down, lying down, lying down. Place a healthy (ideally organic) orange on your sternum against your skin. Close your eyes for a moment. Keep the eye vibration in mind. Be conscious of the vibrations in your body, especially in your chest.

The vibration inside the fruit becomes aware at that point. Draw the vibration of the fruit to enter your own layer of vibration.

Yawning

Yawning is one of the little inner movements that may unexpectedly release enormous amounts of energy. Yawning is the appropriate channel release. As with all channel releases, energy movement is much more vital than physical movement. However, as previously said, this energy transfer must be tolerated. It isn't, or it occurs only seldom. Our ethereal body no longer operates automatically; it is one of those inherent processes.

Boredom abolition is a product of aberrant situations caused by coercive schooling. Boredom, when full, releases the heart, exactly as it cries. It also relieves numerous stresses that would otherwise build up in the eyes, resulting in the little tear that appears in the corner of the eyes after a full and generous yawn.

Let's see how you can make the most of your yawn. When you bend down, most individuals release their energy via their lips, if you look at it from the outside. It will already be a great improvement if you can become conscious of the energy discharge and 'deliberately' enhance it when your bosom.

But there is a better way to yawn. The fundamental idea is to stand up. Instead of being channeled horizontally via the lips, the energy is directed upward toward the top of the head. Every muscle at the back of the neck must be manipulated. While yawning, try to extend the throat.

The mouth should not be too open; in fact, it should be maintained virtually closed. Concentrate your whole concentration on the top of your neck, behind the nasal cavity. This region is intimately related to the metabolism of immortality nectar at the pharyngeal roof.

Tips

If you are quick enough, you may also employ sneezing as an energy release. You've probably observed that yawning is infectious. By using these subconscious forces, a powerful guy might raise his arm, and all the others around him would feel impelled to raise their weapons as well. Yawning is the last remnant of this kind of learning.

Remove any rings you are wearing. Feel the motion in your akin finger.

(That is, if you wear multiple of them, you may test them one at a time).

To intensify the sensation, use throat friction.

The ring will then open, and the eye and finger will become aware of the vibration once again. Stay stationary for about a minute.

Then remove the ring and flip it around. (A ring's two sides, so the side closer to the knuckle is now farther away after you have put the ring on the other side). Slow down and relax into your eye and finger vibrations. Consider throat friction. Compare the vibration to what you experienced the other way around. The ring's vibrational current is often extremely different.

What is the best approach to go about it? Try each position many times until you can determine which ones are correct, 'direct,' and supportive of your forces, and which ones are incorrect.

Tips

Much power may be stored in a ring with or without a mounted stone.

The stronger the ring, the more crucial it is to carry it on the "right side." A pendulum may be used to check the "right" side of the ring.

A Reminder About Being Aware Bracelets! Watches seem far more poisonous to the naked eye than is often assumed. This is especially true with quartz watches: Every vibration of the timepiece sends a whiplash through your etheric body. Even without quartz, all timepieces tend to produce a perverse etheric region and greatly interfere with the normal flow of your energy.

This is an easy test to persuade you that timepieces are harmful.
This experiment is straightforward. A buddy and a pendulum are required for this. A pendulum is ideal for a key or ring strung on a 15 cm (3 inch) cotton thread. It is best to avoid using synthetic thread.

Please have your buddy remove your watch. Hold the pendulum in one hand while taking the correct pulse with the other. This is commonly done by wearing your friend's left watch. If the watch is on the right, you begin by taking the pulse of the left hand.

What is your pulse rate? On the thumb side, just above the bracelet line, place your index, mid-ring, and ring fingers on the radial artery. Please keep in mind that this section of the radial artery is located on the Lung Meridian.

Enter the eye, recognize the vibration, and breathe a little friction while holding the pendulum in one hand and holding the pulse. Then add the pulse energy. Feel for the vibration of the artery. The pendulum's rotation starts in one direction.

Rep the process with your friend's other hand. Increase the vibration of the pulse. In most circumstances, the pendulum will swing the other way. This is a common occurrence: It simply depicts a distinct polarity in the energy of each arm.

Repeat the process after asking your buddy to watch. Take a hand pulse with the watch and tune in! When the watch is below, the pendulum either stops moving or rotates in the other way. That is, the wristwatch cancels or reverses the energy polarity of the arm it is worn on - a startling revelation!

Nothing beats wearing a watch in the proper location on your body.

Nurses' practices of keeping the watch near the heart are strongly discouraged. As long as the watch is in touch with or extremely close to the body (less than 1 or 2 inches distant), it causes significant disturbance in the etheric. As a result, whether you wear your wristwatch or keep it in your pocket, the impact will be the same.

A watch should be kept in a bag rather than on your person. For example, you may connect the watch to the strap of your purse in such a manner that you can read it easily from a distance. Why not experiment with a different look?

CHAPTER 7

SENSITIVITY AND AWARENESS CENTERED ON WATCHFULNESS IN THE EYE

Let us begin with a very modest experience. Close your eyes and form a new link: Be mindful of the friction between your eyes while you breathe. Make your eye vibrate. Then, open your eyes and gaze at everything in front of you. Even if your eyes are open, keep your brows alert to the vibration. What is the scope of your awareness? Your object, as well as the movement of your brows.

There is one item worth noting: It's like looking at something through your brows. You don't have to try; it just occurs. You focus only on an item while being acutely aware of the vibration in your eye. And you're naturally staring at the thing from between your brows. In other words, you're at the right place.

You'll notice that you don't actively seek centeredness; it just occurs. This is due to the third eye's inherent centeredness. As a result, anytime your eye operates, you are focused.

Take another thing and start seeing it. At the same moment, the vibrations between the brows are aware. Another conclusion is that your mind has a tendency to settle down. You don't strive to hush your thoughts. Struggling against the mind to create inner quiet is always futile. Don't do anything; only be aware of the vibration in your eye. As a result, you notice your mind is quieter than normal.

What's up with that? You're already out of mind as soon as you look someone in the eyes. Remember our last eye contact exercise?

We noticed the layer of common sense known as Sanskrit Manas. The façade that constantly talks in your brain is the Manas mind, which is formed of grip and training. The third eye is the door that leads out of the door. So, every time you enter your eye, you take the first step out of your head, which is why everything settles.

Rep to this exercise many times. Choose a few things and spend some time looking at each one. When you have the thing and the vibration/phrasing/pressure is felt between your brows. There you have it. Keep your eyes open and blink as little as possible. Continue to breathe while rubbing your throat. Examine your own awareness and notice how it changes when your eye is not focused.

The eye's central and quiet character reveals the nature of inner alchemy. Outwardness is one of the functions of the eye, according to its anatomy. Enable the structure and put the function in place. Rather than consciously battling your mind to attain inner quiet, you are constructing a new structure, the third eye. Then just alter the structure to enable the function, silence.

This is one of the most important secrets of internal alchemy: Attempt not to solve the issue. Don't spend your time battling your thoughts. The eye, by nature, emanates tranquility after it has been built up. As a result, the objective is to build the third eye in the same way that the ancients constructed churches.

Consider the practice of meditation. You may experience extremely high levels of meditation once or twice in your life, such as when you quit your everyday employment to attend a meditation retreat for a few days or weeks. However, the elevated level of consciousness eventually fades into work and your normal life, and you are caught up in your regular thoughts.

Inner alchemy responds: don't struggle to keep the experience.

You cannot sustain the energy layout that would enable you to stabilize yourself at a higher level of awareness. Such a facility must be built. Start weaving the immortality body. Open the primary energy channel at the center of the body. Make the crown's center at the top of the head.

Create the correct subtle organs, and you will not only be able to experience a consciousness expansion during meditation retreats, but it will also be present at all times. The new condition of consciousness follows you even in the midst of a throng, a crowded railway station, or when driving in traffic. It is not up to your thoughts to stay silent and isolated from the rest of the world. Spiritual knowledge will emanate from the self via the created vehicles, independent of what occurs around you.

We are presently in the process of constructing a third eye in order to complete the first step toward immortality.

Persistence of Vision

Spiritual approaches and practices are many and diverse. They encourage you to look at the world and at yourself from many viewpoints.

However, the majority of them share certain characteristics. The requirement to sustain a continuing interior awareness is central to practically all self-transformation strategies.

Indian gurus often encourage their disciples to consider what distinguishes an enlightened, intelligent person from any other human being. The latter may be brighter, more educated, and more handsome than the wise. He may possess every skill that the intelligent guy lacks.

However, there is one key distinction between the two: The knowledgeable person is always aware, whilst the other is not. The wise man has erupted into a state of spontaneous inner knowing. The other's mind has been captivated by an infinite stream of ideas, perceptions, and emotions that cast a shadow over his Self's vision.

Generations of spiritual innovators have devised a variety of strategies for maintaining this consciousness. Some individuals utilize a mantra, which is a strong series of sounds that they repeat all the time! For example, consider the renowned yogi Ramdas, who attained enlightenment by reciting a 20-year mantra on the Ram. Christian mysticism has analogous practices in the constant repetition of particular prayers. Although it is not for everyone, it may be a highly effective strategy. There are just a few techniques to make a soundtrack repeat indefinitely.

The issue is discovering and sticking to a technique that works with your energies. You may wonder what my magical wall is, which is the technology I use to keep myself aware at all times. Is it effective? This question is critical if you are concerned about your spiritual growth.

You are the answer to the question unless you are not a candidate for higher levels of awareness and initiation. Please keep in mind that you may not always enjoy the proper method at first. Perseverance leads to spiritual prosperity. When you analyze the lives of enlightened gurus, you will see that they often did not comprehend what they were doing. It seemed dry, unproductive, and foreign to the method they were taught, the one via which they subsequently came to light. Why were they masters while so many others were not? They were consistent, consistent, consistent. Persistence became more vital than the approach itself, finally leading to a stunning breakthrough.

You may also walk with the same awareness when you can see an item and are aware of the vibration between your brows. Why don't you give it a shot? Leave your book for a while and take a stroll around, feeling the vibration between your brows.

As a result, this is the first expansion to your daily activities. You may now be a seeker every time you walk. You may either move, get devoured by ideas, or be completely immersed in the vibration between your brows.

Driving is another action that may easily be combined with the awareness in your eye. The site is in harmony, and the spirit is overjoyed. The concentration keeps you alert and concentrated, allowing you to drive for longer periods of time with less stress and weariness. Furthermore, you stay watchful, and your visual angle is wider, which improves driving safety.

The goal is to gradually raise your awareness of your actions until you have a constant eye concentration. This awareness is automatic and easy at first. It is there in all of your behaviors. You are then designated as an initiation candidate.

Consider all the monks who live in a monastery and have nothing to do except pray or think in the morning and evening. Only a handful of them makes it to the light. How can you expect to receive an opportunity if you just meditate once a day for twenty minutes when your life is in turmoil?

The solution is to become more mindful of all of your everyday interactions. Begin to become more aware of your surroundings. The world will then be your teacher rather than your adversary. The worst conditions may be used to evaluate and improve your centeredness and awareness. It is possible to fall asleep in a distinct inner existence in a monastery, which avoids major issues and leads to nothing. If you embrace the world, the world forces you to confront yourself.

Please do not be concerned about being in the eye - have fun! There is a ridiculous way to spend the whole day in your brain, only to recall your wish to watch and get furious because you let your attention wander. Instead of getting eaten by your everyday routines and remembering your attention in your eye just sometimes, I'd advise you to begin by executing certain movements with complete awareness between your brows.

Washing dishes, for example, is completely in the sight. If you put everything inside it, it will become automatic after a few times: once you wash it, the eye will appear on its own. In addition, the use of flowing water throughout the cooking process relieves tensions and false energy and maybe a very pleasant exercise.

Many actions that are often regarded as straightforward and dull will be unexpected if done with your eyes closed. The environment becomes a continual source of astonishment as your eyes grow more attentive and visually focused. You may be aware of where you are right now. It would not be profitable if you quit your work and went into a cave. The issue is not that your work has been altered, but that you are aware of it.

Tips & Tricks for Life in the Eye

There are always a few things to keep in mind: Every time you see them, you return to your concentration. For example, tie a ribbon around your wrist or put little pieces of paper in prominent areas on your walls. Or leave a message for your reflection, or paint a different color on one of your nails.

Doors and gates have a great symbolic significance. A helpful habit is to recall your spiritual desire every time you pass a door.

Another effective method is to get a countdown watch that chimes every seven minutes. When you hear the signal, concentrate for fifteen seconds on the vibration between your brows and breathe through your neck. Seven is an excellent number for self-processing. The signal and practices are repeated with excessive frequency and are not in the duration of the interval. The astral body is rhythmically sensitive, and the habit of looking someone in the eyes is firmly imprinted in you.

Let's try something different. Close your eyes and produce a powerful vibration between your brows by breathing in friction for 1 or 2 minutes. Then, concentrate an d stare into a mirror while opening your eyes and holding your brows.

Of course, addressing them with a humorous look would be difficult for your friends and relatives! So, what should be done? First, practice being in the eye and in the heart every time you talk to someone so that the intensity of the eye is mitigated by the heart's openness and kindness.

Second, after you have established yourself in your sight by actual and consistent practice, your acute semi-frowning will fade and your look will be rather ordinary. In the meanwhile, try to contribute diplomatically.

Permanence assemblage

Let's take a look and attempt to comprehend the benefits of continual awareness.

Consciousness

As previously said, awareness is the most crucial factor. Anyone who is aware is sailing towards Self. Anyone who does not misses out on the fantastic potential for progress.

Centeredness

As the brief experiences at the beginning of this chapter indicated, one of the primary outcomes of being in the eye is a more concentrated state of awareness. There is an essential term in yoga philosophy. Vik Tepa signifies that the situation of the mind is diffused and disseminated. In his Classical Aphorisms on Yoga, the great sage defined Vik talas as one of the most difficult hurdles to spiritual reintegration. The more your eye grows, the more you will be able to keep your thoughts motionless and silent.

Beyond the Discursive Mind Awareness

The benefit of employing the eye with a perspective of awareness is that it leads to vigilance beyond the discursive mind's common level.

When you put yourself on a road of awareness, one of the greatest pitfalls is observing your mind with your mind. Some individuals attain consciousness of their thoughts, but only on a mental level. This implies that whenever you think about your buddy Hilary, you think: "I think about Hilary." This is an example of another idea. That's all there is to it. After a time, these folks are often dissatisfied. They believe they are doing everything correctly, beginning with awareness, yet nothing occurs. They are still laying in their normal state of mind. You will never really enter an enlarged level of awareness.

It is obvious why. The true goal is to become aware of the Self, not merely cognizant of it! Manas, the layer of ordinary mental awareness that constantly speaks in your brain, is the major barrier between you and the Self. The goal is to emerge from the myopic mind into the Self rather than to emulate a higher awareness by adding ideas afterthought.

When you begin to monitor your mind out of mind, your awareness becomes spiritually gratifying. As a result, an awakening of consciousness may be very beneficial: If you follow our teachings, you will be able to break free from the Mana mentality. The most crucial thing is to gaze at auras and non-physical realms "out of mind." You then start living outside of the cage.

You see now why the text has often said that the essential is not what you see, but what you perceive. In terms of spiritual growth, the substance of visions is secondary to the dissolution of the usual layer of mental awareness. People who spend too much time analyzing the symbolic implications of their visions often overlook this.

Create the Eye

By keeping concentrated between the brows, you significantly speed the growth of the eye. Your mind feeds the sight. Furthermore, you develop a connection in order to provide energy and assistance to spiritual guides and assistants. During the early phases of your spiritual growth, it is your responsibility to come and chisel your subtle organs of clarity. Your effort will be substantially aided if you keep continual monitoring. Indeed, the awareness you seek is related. You might say "Keep connected in the eye" instead of "Be aware in the eye." If you concentrate on the formation of a certain length in the eye, the links with your own energy will become more evident.

Persistence in this job induces a number of physiological alterations in the third eye nerves and glans. It is not an energy organ, but rather the third eye itself. It is particularly associated with the Etheric and Astral bodies. However, some physical structures in the region are related to it and will experience dramatic transformations as your awareness progresses, for example, the pineal gland in the future. When discussing the third eye, all occultists mention these two always. An in-depth clear-sighted study, however, reveals that significant changes also occur in other structures such as the ethmoid bone cribriform platform (via which nerves from the narrow mucous membrane reach the brain), the optical chiasma, the frontal air sinuses, the sphenoid air sinuses, and the brain ventricles (fluid-filled cavities).

One of the reasons you can't view the non-physical universe is that your mental mind is overburdened with physical senses. In other words, there's no place for anything else; your mind is crammed with physical sights and noises. The cup must be drained before any material may be placed inside. For example, in Steiner, the apprentice esotericism often discovered that he needed to spend a specific amount of time every day shutting off all sensory awareness. The astral body might then retreat into its own life and search for non-physical pictures. A very similar principle is frequently repeated throughout the numerous yoga's of the Indian tradition. The Sanskrit term pratyahara refers to a retreat from one's senses that permits one to experience a bare state of awareness. Pratyahara is often mentioned in Sanskrit literature as a prerequisite for deeper inner experiences. As you expand your eyesight, you will make an intriguing discovery.

Pollution is a problem of both quantity and quality. It's not only that you're continuously bombarded with physical and sensory sensations that keep you from perceiving other realms. For these bodily impressions, the impact on your system is equally unpleasant. The rough substance gives rise to the bodily senses: They're too coarse; hence, if not filtered, they roughen and unrefined your awareness.

Unprocessed perceptions constantly bombard you: sights, sounds, scents, and so forth. They flood into your thoughts and do considerably more harm than you realize. The fact that the nutrients you ingest have been delivered straight to your body's organs and tissues without being processed by the digestive system serves as an illustration. This would be too "outside-like" if your actual body lost its individuality. That is precisely what occurs to your awareness. She loses her sense of self. The Self is no longer discernible among this flood of external sensations.

I'd want to emphasize this since it seems to be critical when considering the consciousness economy. All sensory inputs, like you, contribute to the weaving of your mental awareness layer. In your day-to-day creation process, a dense cloud of ground astral matter that shields the Self is being formed.

What happens when your third eye remains open? Impression from the outside world is received initially in the third eye rather than directly into your head. Consider the centeredness exercises at the beginning of this chapter, in which you stare at an object while being mindful between your brows. It's like automatically glancing at your third eye, which implies that your visual sensations get there first. So, what exactly is going on? The third eye 'digests' these sensations. It filters and processes them.

This mechanism will strike you as soon as you view it clearly.
The properties of the vibration in your heart fluctuate dramatically depending on whether your third eye has been processed initially. The impressions that came initially via the third eye are smooth and refined. Those who lack are harsh and cacophonous. They're as painful as a headache. You construct your awareness in an unsuitable manner for spiritual consciousness.

Understanding and using this idea is enough to alter one's destiny. What do you notice when you examine your thoughts objectively?

Thoughts are not abstract concepts, but rather a particular substance. This stuff is, of course, not tangible, yet it still exists on some level. And the quality of your thinking is determined by the quality of your intellect. Spiritual or even intelligent ideas cannot develop or be accepted if the mental substrate is gross.
I recommend that you keep this in mind while you work on your spiritual growth.

Practice
You may sit or stand, but keep your back straight. Get mindful between the brows. (You should be raising your brows after reading this chapter!) Get your feet moving. Keep your eyes just moving and blinking.

Pictures

Look around you for an item. Take a look from your eye. Insert the thing between the brows into the eye. Try out the filtering effect we just discussed. Feel the 'weight' of your third eye pictures as if your brows were pushing on them. Make certain that the eye does not get around any visual impact. Keep in mind that the third eye processes all physical pictures.

Close your eyes and become aware. Relax your concentration. As usual, take a mental glance at the things. Look at the difference. Can you notice that your head is less sensitive to vibrations?

Sounds

Use the same sound approach as before. Play some music for one minute without any particular awareness or eye concentration. Try to comprehend the vibrational quality of what is consumed.

Then it becomes aware amid the eyes. Listen with your eyes. Listen with your eyes. Maintain your attention on how the noises in your eye are perceived. Try to notice a change like your inner vibrations.

Smells

Now do something to improve your sense of smell. The chemical first smells without conscious awareness. Then get the stench out of your eyes: stench out of your eyes. How does the input alter when filtered by the eye?

Taste

Begin eating a meal without prior preparation. After a few minutes, the food from the eye starts to taste. The difference in vibration quality is quite noticeable in this scenario.

Selectively practice with different flavors and meals. Compare the effects of sweet, salty, acidic, and other tastes on your eyes one by one.

One significant observation is that you do not always enjoy the same meals when you eat mindlessly.

Practice

Practice walking along the street with your eyes fully focused. Check that your eye gets any picture, sound, or scent. After a few minutes, let go of your awareness. Receive everything mentally, without any concentration in your sight. Examine the vibrational quality inside you. What precisely penetrates you when you experience an image, a sound, or a smell...? What kind of vibration was received? What type of delicate material is introduced to your being?

Repeat your first exercise, but this time emphasize the perceiver, you. Examine a thing without concentrating on it. The thing has certain properties, and there is also some vibration quality inside your skull.

What is added to your vibration when you get the item image? How does the energy level in your mind or elsewhere change? Be more conscious of your surroundings. There are degrees, as far as the eye can see.

You have the option of being 10% or 40% in your eye. And if you keep practicing, one day you will be 100 percent in the eye.

Begin with a little amount in your eye, say 5%. See the difference in the vibration received from the item when no distinct awareness is held inside the eye. Step up 10% in the eye, then 20% in the eye, and so on. Examine the vibration every time you glance at the thing. Then repeat with as much awareness as possible. Consider how you feel about the visual impression. What effect does perception have on your energy? Do you believe the sensory input is astral?

Move from one thing to the next, repeating the observing process with increased eye awareness. Then play some music and repeat the process using sounds this time. You can do the same thing to your taste.

Test

Choose a frenetic location in a huge city. Try to concentrate for half an hour with full sensitivity. Ascertain that there is no perception in the absence of visual processing. Filter even the sensations that are often unnoticed but are nonetheless captured instinctively.

How far can you keep your integrity? Repeat the exam every now and again to monitor your progress.

Vision Alteration

One of the first benefits you will notice when using the strategies taught in this book is a subtle shift in how you perceive space in your daily activities. For the techniques detailed in this part, it would be great if you were outdoors, in a garden, or in a forest.

Examine the trees and necessarily in a meditation pose — simply rest. Just unwind. Make flowers to strengthen your eyes. Sit comfortably, not a connection with your eye between your brows. Keep your eyes peeled. Keep your eyes peeled. It's best not to move too much, but you don't have to assume a statue-like pose like in eye contact.

With eye awareness, resume the tripartite vision process.

The awareness of seeing or seeing. If there are too many visuals, feel the picture rather than look at it.

The Heartfelt Sentiment

While focusing on the eye, you will notice that your perception of the landscape changes gradually. One obvious distinction is that your view is more comprehensive: It incorporates more of the image's periphery. You stay aware of the full image rather than picking one area and automatically concentrating on it. However, peripheral perception has risen significantly. In comparison to what you would ordinarily see, the image looks to be "less flat."

The air seems to 'take size'. There seems to be greater perspective and relief. As your eye develops, this contrast will become more evident. The contrast between a third-eye perspective and a regular vision, or between a holographic image and a flat image, is comparable. Even without including extrasensory perception or aura vision, the eye seems to add a stereoscopic depth to the picture.

Another apparent distinction is that the picture seems to be alive.

The colors seem livelier, as though they have their own intensity and vibrancy. Colors communicate their attributes to your spirit. It gives the whole image a feeling of vibrancy. Suddenly, your physical eyesight improves dramatically: it's as if you've rediscovered the world! All you have to do to access this alternative perspective is to move out of the layer of the mind in which you have been trained to work. Remember, the moment you enter the eye, you're already halfway out of your mind.

When you use regressive methods and vision to re-experience previous life experiences, you learn that until recently, most people experienced the world through this more beautiful and alive vision. The 'flattening' of the field of awareness seems to have begun in the nineteenth century, at the time of the industrial revolution and the exploitation of scientific discoveries. It might be related to what Rudolf Steiner refers to as the emergence of Ahrimanic forces in human awareness.

If you are upset or irritated, I recommend going for a stroll in nature to reconnect with this live vista. It is a peaceful technique to resolve many mental disputes by drawing the beauty of the world from a non-mental viewpoint rather than battling.

The Eye and Heart Consciousness

Once you've established a strong awareness in your eye, the next stage is to anchor it in your heart. I'm not talking about a physical muscular organ, but rather the chakra in the middle of your chest, on the left side of your body. The recommendation was made in numerous eye contacts to put your awareness both in the heart and in the eye as if you were getting pictures and sensations via the eye.

(This holds true throughout the book). This dual concentration will apply to all of your actions.

The awareness of the eye is a development in the focus's third eye. When you know how to live in your eyes, adding the sensation of your heart isn't that tough. The power penetrates more deeply. As a consequence of a greater level of integration, a new palette of sensations and emotions emerges.

What can you see clearly in the aura of someone who has a permanent awareness in both the eye and the heart? Streams of vibration and light begin to circulate about the pulmonary and pineal glands, which are located between the heart and many energy centers.

A new line of communication is built between the heart and the brain. In the energy body, certain new channels are activated. This dual attention varies significantly from the condition of awareness. The fundamental distinction is that awareness in the heart allows you to become closer to your ego or higher Self.

Instead of being separated by awareness, your Self is increasingly receiving your perceptions. Your constant eye attention generates a new style of thinking. This new notion is likewise related to self-presence in the heart.

This twofold attention will undoubtedly increase your awareness of your surroundings. When you are completely aware of your own existence in the heart, you cannot act mechanically or soullessly. You seek to establish a holy connection that will enable the self to accept and express Himself in the world. To put it another way, the big alchemical wedding is being planned: The self and the outside world.

When Should I Start?

When should you start the double eye and concentrate on the single eye? Not too early. Naturally, how much practice you put in will vary.

However, it takes at least 1 to 2 years of constant awareness for your third eye to be completely operational. It would be a major error to stop digging too soon and divert your focus. Even if you feel advanced, I recommend that you continue the one-size-fits-all work in the eye for many months.

We highly advise that after you have achieved eye awareness, you spend one or two days a week just in the eye to enhance it.

There are, however, exceptions to these norms. Certain individuals should focus on the heart rather than the eye from the start of their job because of their own organization, which is the result of previous efforts. For example, when some individuals make touch with their third eye, they are plunged into a frenzy of subtle awareness. They seem to be stretched into astral space. Non-physical entities may be found all over the planet. They merge into spiritual realms and tend to lose sight of themselves. The awareness must be fixed in the middle of the heart in this circumstance.

When such an experience occurs, the focus should be on retaining one's sense of ego and developing self-reference through sensing one's own heart present. The foundation exercises detailed in the protection chapters are also beneficial.

CHAPTER 8

A FEW EXPERIENCES SENSATION IN DIFFERENT PARTS OF THE BODY

In this chapter, we'll look at the most common experiences, sensations, and emotions you could have when working on your eyes and using the methods in the book.

Vibration and tingling indicate that something in your etheric body, a life force layer, is active. It basically states that certain energy rearrangements occur when you meditate on whether pinches occur in your hands, arms, legs, or any other region of your body. For example, certain blocked channels reopen, a specific circulation is briefly enhanced, or some similar movement occurs in the etheric body.

These little symptoms are unimportant in and of themselves. They're on their way, and they shouldn't be too cautious.

Allow things to come and go.

When working with energy, the basic rule is that various sorts of sensations are encountered from time to time. They may include twitches, little discomfort, colors, interior noises, and so forth. You're both coming and departing. They are meaningless unless they become permanent. Until they are permanently removed. Take them as little releases or energy shifts. Stay away from them and go your own path.

If any of them appear often, you must just consider them and attempt to comprehend what they indicate. Is it ever too intense to meditate if the sensation is too strong? It's really contentious! In high-intensity situations, it is essential to remain cool and observe what is occurring without responding.

If you feel uncomfortable and wish to end the experience, just open your eyes and stop practicing. The pressure of the experience instantly reduces as your eyes are opened, and your regular level of awareness is restored.

Higher Vibrations Than Your Eyebrows

A possible sensation is light and pressure on the front of the head, around one inch above the region between the eyes and the front of the skull. Outside of meditation, pressure, and light may be persistent, even if you don't strive to stay vigilant. This pressure indicates that energy is being pushed into your eye. It's like the non-mystical chiseling of your tiny organs of clarity.

Another potential sensation is a shawl of light in the middle of the head (in the top section). A vibrational and mild pressure seems to operate to divide the two hemispheres of the brain.

All of these instances indicate that you are making progress. They are by no means required. You may very easily finish the full opening procedure without feeling them.

Keep an eye out for them if they occur. They take some time and then vanish after this episode is over.

If you wish to aid the process, you might try adjusting the energy behind the force. For example, where does the pressure originate from? Can you sense the presence of any creature behind the sight of light' or anything else you sense? Nothing 'doing' is required. Simply identify the connection that makes it simpler for the assistant to accomplish.

Feeling the Burn

It is possible that heat may be emitted throughout your practice. There is nothing terrible about it. It is frequent at some stages of waking, although it seldom lasts long. If you don't consume alcohol, there's nothing particular you need to do. However, during the heat release time, it is best to avoid eating meat and stick to a spice-based diet as much as possible. Showers may also be used to emit heat into the stream, as in the laundry. Bathing in rivers and seas is also quite acceptable. In Kundalini yoga, it is occasionally advised that the body's warmth be counterbalanced by consuming yogurt in order to release powerful waves of heat. Working on the intake of energy and alcohol is dangerous - this applies to any sort of drink. It paves the way for a slew of destructive energies. No sort of protection can properly safeguard someone who regularly consumes alcohol.

The breath comes to a halt.

It is fairly typical to get the sense that your breath has stopped at some point throughout your meditation. Some individuals are worried.

What if my body didn't restart breathing? You don't have to be concerned since no one has ever died as a result of a natural breath suspension.

The body is aware of what it is capable of! You simply need to wait a few seconds until regular breathing resumes.

Stopping the breath is very valuable. Everything comes to a halt inside, as if in a cosmic standoff. It is a chance to go deeper into space and connect with your enlarged self.

The force in the eye might be painful in certain situations, verging on a headache. It is difficult to deal with eye pressure. What exactly is going on? It is possible to take into account a variety of aspects.

You're Getting a Glimpse of It

You were never taught to concentrate on the third eye, but you are aware of it. However, it is all too easy to get caught up in the conflict and begin to grip the eye rather than be conscious of it. There is unneeded strain, which might lead to headaches.

So, if this occurs to you, have a soft awareness and don't push things.

You are unaware of the energy attempting to pull you up.

As you practice being in the eye, your attention will be raised from the brows up above the head on occasion. The relationship between the third eye and the crown center at the top of the head is extremely natural and intimate. If this occurs, just pull yourself up and enjoy being in over your head for a while. Return to the eye when the event has gone. In the beginning, you may not notice the 'pull' and resist reflexively, holding yourself firmly between the brows. You unknowingly block the natural flow of energy with your drive to keep the proper aspiration in your sight. The end result is straightforward: **A Headache.**

What are our optio ns? The solution is simple: Change your concentration for a while. Move your awareness upward from the brows. The energy that has accumulated in your mind is released. Here's a method for attaining this result.

Control Headaches

Close your eyes and focus on the top of your head approximately 10 cm away. There is an energy center, known as a Chakra, in this location. It is not the crown chakra, but the chakra above it. One of my professors referred to it as "the center of the snake," because when you come into touch with it, you can hear a hissing sound.

Set yourself in the 3–5-inch space above your head and spend one minute being alert and listening. Remember, no fantasy! Being just aware is preferable to making a sound.

For a minute or two, keep your awareness at the same height, around 15 cm above the top of your head, while making a constant hissing sound. Hiss as though you were a giant serpent, not merely repeat. Put all into the music while keeping your brain aware. Then, for 2 or 3 minutes above your head, softly repeat the sound inside yourself.

In many cases, you will be astonished at how quickly your headache will go. The more you practice this method, the more unpleasant energy you will be able to release over your head.

Tips

- A dab of tiger balsam on the forehead may help with energy-related headaches, especially when administered early on.

- When moving energy up through the skull is challenging, consider transferring it via the rear of the skull rather than the middle. At the bai hui acupuncture point, this zone is simpler to get out of the mind.

- To aid the upward circulation of the energies, elevate your brows from the beginning to the completion of this operation.

- This approach allows 'over-practice' to relieve strain on the brain. However, once you've mastered the procedure, you can get rid of practically any headache, even if it was caused by something completely unrelated. The technique may be utilized to regulate migraines from all backgrounds, as long as the patient is willing to learn how to use energy.

-

Additional Possible Headache Causes

Let us consider a few more probable causes of headaches in our internal alchemy work (note that this does not include all headaches caused by medical ailments).

- If you meditate or work on a toxic earth line, you may experience a variety of negative symptoms, including headaches.

- You may possibly reveal these symptoms, which aggravates them. Expand your horizons. It's not that you make yourself worse, but that you become more aware of your energy imbalance. You may save yourself a lot of trouble in the long run by addressing the issue (moving your bed, for example).

- Meditation or sleeping near the fridge, TV, electric heater, wires, electric blankets, electronic equipment, or synthetic tapestries might also create capital dysfunctions. The removal of the source eliminates headaches.

- To summarize, apart from the aforementioned reasons, headaches from operating on the eye are uncommon. If you experience headaches and have eliminated all of the aforementioned possibilities, the issue is most likely caused by something other than your spiritual practice. In this scenario, it is important to consult with a medical professional.

Dizziness

There is nothing wrong with feeling a little light after certain practices that take you out into the world. In an extended level of awareness, you feel exceedingly light and a bit euphoric, as if you had one or two glasses of champagne. However, you are not always lightheaded; some are 'heavy-headed!' It is not always the case! In the typical discursive mind, life generates a stifling heaviness of ideas and sensations. People, however, are oblivious to it because they have been conditioned for so long.

As you grow, you will find that a mild sensation of lightness becomes 'natural' and integrates into your typical working technique. You're not going to notice anything. Even though you feel a bit 'weird' at first, you will quickly be able to function from this lightness more easily and efficiently. If the light-headed experience becomes unpleasant for whatever reason, the following solutions will most likely immediately restore the situation:

To establish a strong awareness of your eye and belly, do the grounding techniques described in the previous chapters. (It's an incredible delight to soar in your shoes once you start working with angels.)

Eat! Food is one of the few methods to lay a solid foundation quickly. If a buddy is completely spaced out after meditation and there is an urgent cause to bring him back, feed him. Cakes and even meat are alternatives to heavy meals in an emergency. But don't overdo it: Grounding should come from your power mastery, not a shaky diet! This is quite effective!

Getting Tired

What happens if you become tired or upset as a result of your meditation? So, what happens? The first piece reveals your emotional barriers. This makes it logical and is required. When you strive to refine and purify your system, you uncover all that is unclear within, allowing you to liberate and repair it. These obstructions function similarly to spreading in your astral body. When you clear them, you will often see significant improvements in your perspective opening.

If emotional release strategies are unavailable, vigorous physical activity may be beneficial. Gardening and agricultural activities are also quite relaxing. However, keep in mind that even if you feel better after completing physical exercises, no issues will be cured.

You must use proper strategies to delve deeper into your mind's conflicts. Ignoring the task of emotional cleansing is probably the major reason why some individuals pursue meditation or an evolutionary process for thirty years or more with no significant breakthrough.

Sound Recognition

Listening to non-physical noises is a common travel experience. It usually starts with a buzzing sound in your mind and gradually refines the harmony of the spheres. Only listen to them if you have noises in your mind. They are a terrific focus to keep you alert. The optimum place to position your awareness to change into non-physical sounds is behind the brows in the middle of the head.

If there is no energy, energy must be found somewhere! On certain days, the energy connection is strong and flows effortlessly and spontaneously. There seems to be no energy for other days, and it is much more difficult to immerse oneself in the experience.

The nature of energy varies. For example, the vibration is particularly strong around the Full Moon, but it is sometimes not felt around the New Moon. The violet area of the third eye is frequently easier to reach around the New Moon. Many more energy fluctuations may be seen, some of which are predicted and others which are not. Perhaps one day, a reliable "energy meteorology" will be discovered. That is the goal of true astrology.

To be successful in your practice, you must learn to sense and deal with these fluctuations. For example, if you have one of these days when you are instantly projecting into purple space as soon as you shut your eyes, you should not spend your time fighting for clean channel releases since the frequency cannot be felt anyhow. Concentrate on meditation and attempt to go as far into space as possible. Often, this does not indicate a lack of energy in your practice, but rather that you are seeking it in the incorrect place. Adjust and attempt to touch a higher layer; what you discover may surprise you.

Tamas comes after Sattva. Rajas is fighting Tamas.
In Indian tradition, all manifestations of the creation are evaluated in terms of the three modalities of nature known as tamas, rajas, and sattva. Tamas represents lethargy, opacity, dullness, a lack of initiative, and a feeling of sloth.

Rajas is an exercise that includes movement and wishful thinking. When Radar is triggered in you, you begin to rush about and follow things you desire; you get highly interested in the pursuit of the world. Excessive rajas cause agitation and restlessness.

Pure and transparent states create consciousness and perceptual openness, sensitivity to light, and greater awareness in Sattva. Spiritual growth may be seen as the sattva's inward unfoldment in order to represent yourself.

One of the essential rules of the interaction of the three gu-toas is that tamas (inertia) are triggered after a large dosage of sattva (clearness). In practice, this implies that feeling inert and confused following an extremely clear experience of awareness is perfectly common for a time. Re-entry into a sattva's inner realm is tough under these tamasic circumstances. First, a Radar changeover will be considerably simpler, and your saliva may then be searched for again. This implies that if you feel unreceptive the day after a stunning awakening, it is preferable not to attempt to meditate for lengthy amounts of time. It is preferable to move for a longer period of time: go for a stroll in the countryside, perform some physical labor, and try to be as awake as possible. You may then restart your search for clarification.

www.ingramcontent.com/pod-product-compliance
Lightning Source LLC
LaVergne TN
LVHW050628200726
843506LV00010B/1164